KNOWING YOUR
GRANDFATHER
Joseph William Wilson
1879–1958

BY THE SAME AUTHOR

Marchmont in Edinburgh 1984

Villages of Edinburgh Volume 1 (North) 1986

Villages of Edinburgh Volume 2 (South) 1987

Edinburgh: Sciennes and the Grange 1990

Yerbury: A Photographic Collection 1850–1993 1994

Edinburgh: Gorgie and Dalry 1995

Villages of Edinburgh: An Illustrated Guide Volume 1 (North) 1997

The District of Greenbank in Edinburgh 1998

Villages of Edinburgh: An Illustrated Guide Volume 2 (South) 1999

Old Tollcross, Morningside and Swanston 2001

Marchmont, Sciennes and the Grange 2001

Old Dalry in Edinburgh 2002

Old Gorgie 2002

Edinburgh from the Air: 70 Years of Aerial Photography 2003

Old Dean and Stockbridge 2004

KNOWING YOUR
GRANDFATHER
Joseph William Wilson
1879–1958

Malcolm Cant

MALCOLM CANT PUBLICATIONS

First published in 2004 by

Malcolm Cant Publications
13 Greenbank Row
Edinburgh EH10 5SY

ISBN 0 9526099 7 5

British Library Cataloguing-in-Publication Data
A catalogue record for this book is available on request

Book and cover designed by Mark Blackadder

Printed and bound by The Cromwell Press,
Trowbridge, Wiltshire UK

CONTENTS

Joseph William Wilson and his wife, Mary Jane, with their daughter, Jean *c.* 1908

PREFACE AND ACKNOWLEDGMENTS

Joseph William Wilson was born at 7.30 pm on Wednesday, 18 June 1879 at Creewood Cottage, Minnigaff, Kirkcudbrightshire, and died, aged 78, at 1.40 pm on Thursday, 16 January 1958 at the Longmore Hospital, Salisbury Road, Edinburgh. Joseph spent most of his adult life in what is usually known as the South Side of Edinburgh, in a very different environment from the one into which he had been born. His forebears had worked on the land for many generations in the south-west of Scotland: he was the only one to venture to the east side of the country.

Joseph's paternal grandfather, Thomas Wilson, was born *c.* 1801 and died on 19 June 1880, aged 79, at Craigoch shepherd's house, a few miles north of New Luce. His marriage to Agnes Davidson produced ten children: Agnes, Thomas, Joseph, John, William, Robert, James, Mary, Ronald and Adam, names which recur in the family in later generations.

Thomas, the second child of Thomas and Agnes, was Joseph's father, born on 19 May 1832 at Green, Barr, in Ayrshire, who spent all his life as a Galloway shepherd in the south-west of Scotland. He married the blacksmith's daughter, Annie McGowan (born 1846), on 13 June 1871 at Palnure, the union producing nine children – six boys and three girls. Joseph's father died at Cairnholy on 24 July 1908 and his mother died, also at Cairnholy, on 6 July 1916, aged 70. On the basis of Thomas' known date of birth and date of death, taken from the official records, he was 76 when he died but his death certificate and his tombstone in the kirkyard at Kirkmabreck Parish Church in Creetown say 73.

When Thomas and Annie married, he was 38 and she was 25. Again there is an age discrepancy: their marriage certificate gives Thomas' age as 36. Their nine children were produced in fairly quick succession, the first when Annie was 26 and the last when she was 42. The children were: Thomas, born 1872; John, 1874; James, 1875; Margaret (Maggie or Peggie), 1877; Joseph William, 1879; Robert, 1881; Annie, 1883; William, 1886; and Agnes Davidson, 1888. It was a healthy strain: the average age at death of the nine children was 82.

With a large family, the frequent birth records help the researcher to track most of the addresses where the family lived. In addition to that, the national census, completed at ten-year intervals from 1841 (excluding 1941) provides highly detailed information on the country's population. At the time of writing, the most recent census available to the public is 1901. Using a combination of information from birth, marriage, and death certificates, the national census, Valuation Rolls and family knowledge, it is possible to put together something of the life and family background of Joseph William Wilson which, I think, helps those of us who knew him to understand more of what we remember, and, hopefully, for those who never knew him, to have some appreciation of his life and times. I have not set out to complete a family tree which is already being done very ably by William Taylor, who kindly allowed me to extract various names and dates from his research for use in this book. William's grandfather and my grandfather were brothers. My goal was to piece together as much information as I could on the life of my grandfather, Joseph William Wilson, from his birth in 1879 at Minnigaff to his death in 1958 in Edinburgh. In doing so, of course, I also researched the family background of Mary Jane Mathieson Kain, my grandmother, who married Joseph William Wilson in Edinburgh in 1904. The information now available to us on the Kain family at Dumfries, Hawick and Selkirk is something of a revelation and is dealt with in detail in Chapters 4 and 5.

In putting together this brief reconstruction of my grandfather's life I have derived a great deal of assistance from the extended family, many other individuals in Edinburgh and throughout the south of Scotland, and several libraries, archives and other repositories of information. They are mentioned in the text but, in case I have omitted some, I acknowledge their assistance here. I also thank the people who have made the production of this book possible: Nicola Wood edited the script to her usual high standard; Oula Jones compiled the index; Mark Blackadder designed the book and jacket; and Neville Moir supervised all aspects of production.

Just what my grandfather would say about the following pages is not ours to know. It is even possible that he was not aware of some of the infomation now available to us.

Malcolm Cant FCII, FSA (Scot.)

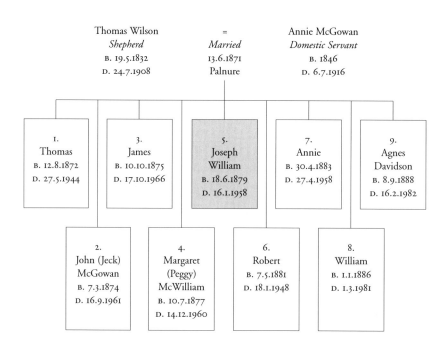

Thomas Wilson	=	Annie McGowan
Shepherd	*Married*	*Domestic Servant*
B. 19.5.1832	13.6.1871	B. 1846
D. 24.7.1908	Palnure	D. 6.7.1916

1. Thomas	3. James	5. Joseph William	7. Annie	9. Agnes Davidson
B. 12.8.1872	B. 10.10.1875	B. 18.6.1879	B. 30.4.1883	B. 8.9.1888
D. 27.5.1944	D. 17.10.1966	D. 16.1.1958	D. 27.4.1958	D. 16.2.1982

2. John (Jeck) McGowan	4. Margaret (Peggy) McWilliam	6. Robert	8. William
B. 7.3.1874	B. 10.7.1877	B. 7.5.1881	B. 1.1.1886
D. 16.9.1961	D. 14.12.1960	D. 18.1.1948	D. 1.3.1981

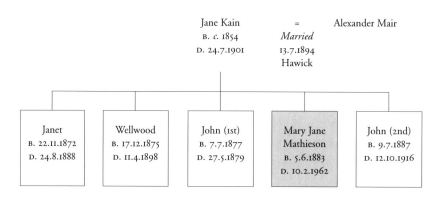

Jane Kain	=	Alexander Mair
B. *c.* 1854	*Married*	
D. 24.7.1901	13.7.1894	
	Hawick	

Janet	Wellwood	John (1st)	Mary Jane Mathieson	John (2nd)
B. 22.11.1872	B. 17.12.1875	B. 7.7.1877	B. 5.6.1883	B. 9.7.1887
D. 24.8.1888	D. 11.4.1898	D. 27.5.1879	D. 10.2.1962	D. 12.10.1916

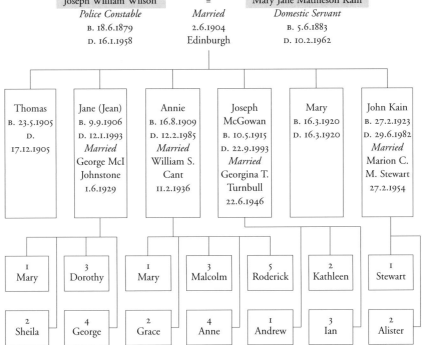

Joseph William Wilson
Police Constable
B. 18.6.1879
D. 16.1.1958

=
Married
2.6.1904
Edinburgh

Mary Jane Mathieson Kain
Domestic Servant
B. 5.6.1883
D. 10.2.1962

Thomas
B. 23.5.1905
D.
17.12.1905

Jane (Jean)
B. 9.9.1906
D. 12.1.1993
Married
George McI
Johnstone
1.6.1929

Annie
B. 16.8.1909
D. 12.2.1985
Married
William S.
Cant
11.2.1936

Joseph
McGowan
B. 10.5.1915
D. 22.9.1993
Married
Georgina T.
Turnbull
22.6.1946

Mary
B. 16.3.1920
D. 16.3.1920

John Kain
B. 27.2.1923
D. 29.6.1982
Married
Marion C.
M. Stewart
27.2.1954

1
Mary

3
Dorothy

1
Mary

3
Malcolm

5
Roderick

2
Kathleen

1
Stewart

2
Sheila

4
George

2
Grace

4
Anne

1
Andrew

3
Ian

2
Alister

LIST OF ILLUSTRATIONS

c. 1905   1908   1920s

1930s   1930s   1947

1951   1950s   1957

THE MINNIGAFF CONNECTION

Most of my adult life I have been aware that my grandfather came from Minnigaff, Kirkcudbrightshire. I remember, particularly, the subject being discussed when I took my mother to visit her Aunt Agnes (my grandfather's sister) at Newton Stewart Hospital in 1981. As my mother and I were leaving Newton Stewart over the Cree Bridge she pointed down to the left towards Minnigaff and said that that was where her father had been born. She was keen to go and look for the cottage but there was insufficient time to do so. However, more than twenty years later, after studying marriage and birth certificates, it now seems to me that Creewood Cottage in Minnigaff was the first matrimonial home of Joseph's parents, Thomas and Annie, who married in 1871. Their first child, Thomas, was born at Creewood Cottage in 1872, John in 1874, James in 1875, Maggie in 1877, then Joseph William in 1879, followed by Robert in 1881. As the seventh child, Annie, was born in 1883 at Lochton, near Barrhill, the family were at Creewood Cottage from 1871 to a date sometime after 7 May 1881 (when Robert was born) but moved before 30 April 1883 when Annie was born. On the evidence of the birth certificates alone, Creewood Cottage was a very important location in the family history.

Early in April 2003 I decided to spend a couple of days in Newton Stewart and Minnigaff to see if I could locate Creewood Cottage. I left my car in the main street of Newton Stewart anticipating that a search on foot was likely to be more productive. However, it was soon evident that the distances involved were such that I would have to drive. As I was walking back to the car, I saw three people chatting over a garden wall who looked as though they were locals. I discovered that they were knowledgable about the area but had never heard of Creewood Cottage. As I was about to take my leave, another man came by who was seized upon by the group, metaphorically speaking, and quizzed about the name Creewood Cottage. The gentleman, Robert Smith, had no difficulty remembering the cottage but said that it had been demolished many years ago. After taking instructions on how to find the site I set off up the Creewood road, full of expectation. Stopping to check my progress a few miles on, I noticed a chap burning wind-blown timber in the woods, and shouted over to him. On asking him if he knew where Creewood Cottage was, he answered: 'You're too late, I demolished it years ago.' Ian Gillespie told me that he had not known it previously but that in 1967 or 1968 he was employed to use a JCB to demolish the derelict cottage. He remembered it as being of modest construction, probably only two main rooms, and, at the time, almost roofless and in poor condition. After demolition, the stones were scattered and left on the site, but the slates were saved and used later on the roof of a house known as Blair's Croft, near Creetown. Ian also remembered that there was an interesting lintel stone over the window with the name Creewood and a scroll carved in the stonework, either on one side or both sides of the lintel. Although we had only just met, Ian and I got on well and we joked about the coincidence of stopping at that point and why he had not phoned me before knocking down the house in which my grandfather was born.

Ian gave me clear instructions on how to locate the site and I set off again. Within about two miles I found the small bridge over the burn, a few yards before Drannandow Farm road end where the surrounding land was so overgrown that I could not detect the presence of any building materials on the ground. I saw the sign for Drannandow (which I recalled was the name on the birth certificate of one of the other siblings) and decided to explore further. I enquired at the farm house where I met Robert Horne. Without hearing my story first, he asked me into his house and introduced me to his wife, Jean. I remember saying to them that they would be wondering why a total stranger from Edinburgh was coming into their house unannounced. Mrs Horne's reply, so typical of trusting country people, was: 'Aye, but I expect you are going to tell us.' When I began to relate my interest in Creewood Cottage, Mrs Horne got up from her chair,

Creewood Cottage, photographed from the south, in June 1949. The bridge carries the road over the Coldstream Burn which runs into the River Cree to the left of the picture.
Courtesy of Mrs Jean Ross, née Carlyle.

Creewood Cottage in June 1949, showing the carved stone with the name 'Creewood' in the apex above the square window. There may have been a date stone above the carved stone. The bridge over the Coldstream Burn is on the left. *Courtesy of Mrs Jean Ross, née Carlyle.*

and, without saying a word, went 'ben the hoose'. She came back with a framed water colour painting – of Creewood Cottage. I couldn't believe my luck. There it was, a small single-storey cottage on the left-hand side of the road immediately beyond the small bridge over the burn and before Drannandow road end. All was revealed. According to the painting, Creewood Cottage was clearly between the road and the River Cree and not on the opposite side of the road where I had been looking. I had misunderstood Ian Gillespie's directions. While we were chatting about when the cottage was demolished I started to make a rough sketch of its outline, at which point Mrs Horne said I could keep the painting if I would like to have it. Apparently, just a few weeks before my arrival, the painting had been given to them by an acquaintence who had bought it at a sale in Gatehouse. There was still more to follow.

Earlier that day I had been advised to find Lex Murray who had known the cottage and knew the area well. When I mentioned Lex's name, Robert said that he was shooting foxes up on the hill and that his car was parked beside mine in the yard. Robert went out and left a note on Lex's windscreen and about fifteen minutes later he appeared at the door. He clearly remembered the cottage and the Carlyle family who were the last occupants. When Lex described the cottage as having a scrolled lintel with the name Creewood, Robert suddenly remembered that the stone had been saved and that he thought it had lain about the steadings of Drannandow Farm. I sensed that we were not going to start a search there and then but privately I was hoping that the lintel stone would be found one day so that I could get a photograph of it.

After we had all had tea and biscuits Lex and I went down to the site of Creewood Cottage. It was a strangely emotional experience on a beautiful still April evening. We ferreted about in the trees and undergrowth and could feel the outline of the abandoned stones underfoot but there was nothing discernible above ground other than a short section of what looked like a ruinous dry-stane garden dyke. Nearer to the River Cree the ground was flat and more open, giving the impression that it might have been a vegetable garden at one time. The small burn ran past the house and was no doubt the only source of water at one time. On the opposite side of the road and at a slightly higher level was a strongly built stone outhouse which Lex said had been used as a byre associated with

Lex Murray at the site of Creewood Cottage on 3 April 2003, the birthplace of Joseph William Wilson on 18 June 1879.

Jean and Robert Horne at Drannandow Farm, 2000, where the Creewood stone was located in 2003.

Creewood Cottage. Before leaving, Lex took my photograph at the point where the door to the house would have been and I also took his photograph at the same spot. From a 'cold' start only a few hours earlier, I had learned more about Creewood Cottage by talking to seven or eight people than I would have got from any number of official forms.

As always, of course, there is a down side to research, although the euphoria of the moment was preventing me from even acknowledging it. Later in the evening I was going over my notes for the day and kept coming back to the information on the reverse of the Creewood Cottage painting. Instead of saying Creewood Cottage as I had hoped and expected, it had two names, neither of which I recognised. The writing did not seem to be by the same hand nor written at the same time. What looked like the older of the two inscriptions said 'Old Penninghame Lodge in Wood off Cree Road', and an extra label said 'Cruives End Cottage'. This was potentially disappointing even although the authenticity of the painting was not in doubt and the topography was exactly accurate. I can't say that I had a sleepless night but I was more than pleased to have the doubt resolved the following day when I met Jim McLay of The Museum in Newton Stewart. Jim was very interested in the painting and had no difficulty explaining the other two names. To begin with, he was sure that the word 'off' should have read 'of'. As a retired headmaster, it was not the first time that he had made a similar observation. Jim explained that Creewood Cottage was on the opposite bank of the River Cree to Penninghame House, but in the absence of a bridge over the River Cree there was no possibility of Creewood Cottage being a lodge house to Penninghame unless there was also a ferry – and there was no evidence of that. However, Jim was able to advise me that on Ainslie's map of 1782 a road is shown crossing the River Cree at Penninghame House, which could have been by either a ford or a bridge. There is also a suggestion of a crossing on Johnstone's map of 1820 but, disappointingly, there is no crossing shown on the 1847 Ordnance Survey map. Several people in the locality of Creewood have also spoken of a rope bridge across the river at this point. It is possible, therefore, that Creewood Cottage could, at one time, have been one of the lodges to Penninghame House. The explanation for the second name 'Cruives End Cottage' was equally interesting. The word Cruives refers to a stretch of the River Cree slightly upstream from the position of Creewood Cottage where it is wide, almost like a loch, and the word 'cruives' is used to describe a method of catching salmon. The description Cruives End Cottage therefore explains exactly the position of Creewood Cottage.

There was, of course, another strong lead which needed to be followed up and that was in relation to the Carlyle family who were believed to have been the last occupants of Creewood Cottage. I did not have much to go on, but Mollie McWhirter of Minnigaff patiently made several phone calls for me which located Jean Carlyle who had lived at Creewood Cottage with her mother and father. Jean very kindly replied to my correspondence and provided photographs and additional information. The photographs were further confirmation that the house in the painting was Creewood Cottage: indeed, one of the photographs had been taken from exactly the same position as the painting, with the old bridge in the foreground.

Jean's description of the cottage is based on her childhood residence there between 1944 and 1954, whereas Joseph William Wilson was born there much earlier, in 1879. Nevertheless, there are several aspects which, in all probability, had not changed greatly from around 1881 when the Wilsons left to 1944 when the Carlyles arrived. Creewood Cottage, the shepherd's house for Drannandow Farm, was situated almost three miles from Minnigaff on the minor road to Bargrennan. It was a single-storey, slated dwelling of granite blocks, with floors of sandstone flags, and diamond-paned windows. On the front of the building, above the living-room window, was a lintel stone with the name 'Creewood' cut into it, but there was no date. The entrance porch, only a few yards from the roadside, gave access, on the right, to a small room used as the milk house and pantry, and, on the left, to the main living-room of the house. The only form of heating was a black range open fire with an oven on the left-hand side. The fire was lit almost every day as it was required for cooking and also for heating water in large kettles and pans. Usually coal was used to fuel it during the day and logs in the evening. There was no electricity or gas, nor running water. The living-room gave access to a small kitchen on the left-hand side of the house, and also to two bedrooms, the larger one to the back of the house and the smaller one to the rear of the milk house and pantry. The very small kitchen, with a wooden work top but no sink, had a door to the garden where there was a dry toilet and a place to wash clothes. Water for washing clothes and dishes was scooped up with a

NAME OF CHILD.	SEX.		NAME OF FATHER.	MAIDEN NAME OF MOTHER
	Male.	Female.		
Alexander	M	—	Jagnes McGuffie	Elizabeth Quig
William	M	—	James Graham	Mary Skinning
Marya Paterson Chisholm	—	F.	John McDowall	Mary Chisholm
Mary McCleary	—	F	John Kellie	Jeanie Hervey
Lessie	—	F	John Kelly	Elizabeth Walker
John	M	—	Andrew Christie	Elizabeth McKerlie
Joseph – William	M	—	Thomas Wilson	Annie McGowan
Alexander Murray	M	—	Thomas Wilson	Elizabeth Sillar
Margaret Brown	—	F	David Wilson	Sarah Neill
			Robert Fulton	Agnes Laurie
			John McQuaker	Jane Ross
			Robert Beattie	Agnes Love
			John Corson	Henrietta Skinning
			William Mary	Sarah Michael
			Herbert Snow Ingram	Margaret Jane Gram
			James Wilson	Maggie Parker
			Thomas McDavid	Elizabeth McGeor
			Robert Armstrong	Janet Storey
			William Wilson	Janet Waugh
			Thomas Hannah	Agnes Witham
			Alexander McRae	Isabella Clarke
			Joseph McDavid	Isabella McClymo

Thomas Wilson, the author's great-grandfather,
was born on 19 May 1832 at Barr, Ayrshire. He
married Annie McGowan in 1871 at Palnure and
died on 24 July 1908 at Cairnholy. They had six
sons and three daughters.
Courtesy of Mrs Grace Thom, née Cant.

Employment or Profession of Father	Date of Birth.		Where Born—Parish, Place, Town or Street.	Date of Baptism.		By Whom Baptised.
	1879			1879		
cultural Labourer	May	28	Kirkmabreck; Palnure	June	30	M. S. S. J.
ed Miner	May	29	Kirkmabreck; Palnure	June	30	M. S. S. J.
Gardener	June	8	Minnigaff; Bkeraig	July	6	M. S. S. J. (In Session)
Shepherd	June	4	Minnigaff; Littlepark	July	7	M. S. S. J.
Dairyman	June	5	Minnigaff; Larg	July	8	M. S. S. J.
Gardener	May	11	Minnigaff; Bargalie Lodge	July	11	M. S. S. J.
Shepherd	June	18	Minnigaff; Creewood Cottage	July	14	M. S. S. J.
Tinner	June	23	Penninghame; Newton-Stewart	July	25	M. S. S. J.
ed Miner	July	13	Minnigaff; Littlepark	August	4	M. S. S. J.
Butler	July	6	Minnigaff; Cairnsmore			
Dairyman	August	4	Minnigaff; Machremore			
ead Miner	September	4	Minnigaff; Bkeraig			
Wrchhend	Sept.	20	Minnigaff; Machleane			
ad Miner	Sept.	3	Minnigaff; Bkeraig			
Merchant	Sept.	11	Minnigaff; Creebridge			
ster-Gardener	Sept.	30	Penninghame; Newton-Stewart			
Sawyer	Sept.	26	Penninghame; N. Stewart			
ation Master	Oct.	19	Minnigaff; Palnure			
Shepherd	October	26	Minnigaff; Creebridge			
ad Miner	Oct.	12	Minnigaff; Bkeraig			
eneral Labourer	Nov.	18	Minnigaff; Bkeraig			
ilor (Journeyman)	Nov.	3	Newton-Stewart; Queen Street			

The Birth and Baptismal Register for Minnigaff Parish for the year 1879 confirms that Joseph William Wilson was baptised by the Rev. M. S. S. Johnstone on Monday, 14 July 1879, probably at Creewood Cottage.

Monigaff Parish Church, photographed from the ruins of the medieval church in 2003. *Photograph by Phyllis M. Cant.*

shallow basin from a gravel pool formed in the burn. Clothes were washed in the open air in a large boiler, the water being heated by a small fire underneath. The clothes were then gathered in a zinc bath and put through the mangle, or wringer, before being hung out to dry. The cottage had a fairly extensive garden running down to the River Cree which occasionally flooded but never as far as the house. There was sufficient space for a large drying green, a vegetable bed, fruit bushes and a pig sty in the far corner. The stone-built byre (already mentioned) on the opposite side of the road was sufficiently big to house two milking cows and their calves, which, in the summer months, had to be driven to and from grazing fields near Drannandow Farm. Hay was stacked nearby to provide winter forage.

Jean described life at Creewood Cottage in the 1940s as 'decidedly primitive' compared to modern standards of living. Perhaps the most arduous task was to bring drinking water from the spring which was about quarter of a mile from the cottage. The spring was situated on higher ground beyond old lead mines which at one time had been a feature of the district.

When Jean lived at the cottage she attended Minnigaff School, cycling a total of six miles every day. During snowy weather her mother kept her off and when it was wet she would take extra clothing which she could change into when she got to school.

Shortly after meeting Jean Carlyle I was fortunate to be put in touch with Jim Logan whose mother Davida Logan (née Stewart) and uncle, Bob Stewart, had lived at Creewood Cottage in the 1920s. I interviewed Mrs Logan at Newton Stewart in June 2003. Davida was able to confirm almost all the information already provided by Jean Carlyle, particularly the description of the cottage, its accommodation, and its lack of facilities. She remembered the stone with the name Creewood and thought that there might also have been a date stone from the early 1800s. Davida lived at Creewood Cottage from 1926 to 1930 with her mother, father, sister and three brothers. Like Jean, Davida found that fetching drinking water from the spring further up the hillside was one of the most arduous tasks. The

OPPOSITE. The Rev. Michael Shaw Stewart Johnstone, minister of Monigaff Parish Church, was born on 14 May 1811 at Berwick-upon-Tweed. He introduced the first organ in the district to Monigaff Parish Church in 1873. In 1876 his parishioners donated £300 to have his portrait painted by Sir Francis Grant, from which this reproduction has been taken.
Courtesy of Monigaff Parish Church.

source of drinking water was not a sunk well but a small hollowed-out rocky area where spring water had been piped to make collection easier. Only two families used the water: the Stewarts at Creewood and the Scotts nearby, the local gamekeeper's family. Mrs Stewart got most of her family provisions from Tom Hannah's van, which called weekly. The system was that each household put in an order the week before, which could include bread, flour, oatmeal and small kitchen utensils like bowls and other crockery.

For the children, the walk to school was often tiring and sometimes character-building, especially on very hot or wet days when the children of better-off families passed by in the comfort of a pony and trap. Unlike today, young children were considered completely safe walking along a quiet country road to school. About the only cause for mild concern was when the young group passed by a well-known local tramp, known affectionately as Heather Jock, who had a rather fierce expression but was otherwise quite harmless.

The school route taken by Jean Carlyle and the Stewart children would have been substantially similar to that taken by Joseph's older brothers in the 1880s, except that the journey for the Wilson family was quite a bit longer. When the Wilsons were at Creewood Cottage, Minnigaff School had not yet been built, and Creebridge Public School, which they attended, was about half a mile further on.

Having heard first-hand accounts of walking three miles to and from school each day, it was all the more interesting to discover that the Admissions and Withdrawals Register, 1865–1906, for Creebridge Public School survives and is available for consultation at Ewart Public Library in Dumfries. I knew that the six oldest Wilson siblings, Thomas, John, James, Margaret, Joseph and Robert were all born at Creewood, which suggested that at least the older ones would be listed. In fact, Thomas is the only member of the Wilson family who is definitely included. He was admitted to Creebridge Public School on 15 September 1878, at age 5 and left on 15 April 1881 at age 8. His date of birth is given as 12 September 1872 whereas his birth certificate says 12 August 1872. There is also reference to a John Wilson, son of Thomas Wilson of Drannandhu, but the date of birth and date of leaving clearly do not relate to Joseph's brother, John McGowan Wilson. The explanation could be that two pupils with the same surname,

Wilson, have been confused. The date of leaving school for Thomas is, however, significant as it must indicate fairly accurately the date on which the Wilsons left Creewood. Robert was born at Creewood on 7 May 1881 and James (born on 10 October 1875) was not registered at all at Creebridge Public School, although he would have been six years of age in October 1881. It seems likely, therefore, that the Wilsons left Creewood in the second half of 1881, presumably on one of the term days when farm employees moved to other employers: Lammas, on 1 August, or Martinmas, on 11 November. The remaining Wilson siblings (Margaret, Joseph and Robert) were all under school age in 1881 and would not, therefore, have appeared in the register. In addition to the Admissions and Withdrawals Register, Ewart Public Library holds the log book for Creebridge Public School between 1873 and 1906. School log books were usually written up each day but they seldom referred to individual pupils by name. They do, however, give a general picture of particular aspects of a school at a given date. During 1878, when Joseph's oldest brother, Thomas, was beginning school, there are three interesting entries: 'two [pupils] from 3rd Standard left to go to Ewart Ragged School; School Inspection, present 44 boys and 41 girls; no school Thursday and Friday [18 and 19 April] being the Sacramental fast day in the Parishes of Minnigaff and Penningham.'

During my visit to Newton Stewart and Minnigaff, Jim McLay also introduced me to Margaret Shankland of Palnure who is actively involved in The Museum and Monigaff Parish Church. She had copies of Monigaff Parish Church baptismal records and was able to show me entries for my grandfather and also his younger brother, Robert. Joseph's entry confirms that he was born to Thomas Wilson, shepherd, and his wife, Annie McGowan (maiden name) on 18 June 1879 at Minnigaff, Creewood Cottage and was baptised on 14 July 1879 by the Rev. M. S. S. Johnstone. Similar information appears for Joseph's younger brother, Robert, born on 7 May 1881 and baptised by the same minister on 16 May 1881. Joseph's day of baptism was a Monday, as was Robert's, which seems to confirm that the more common practice in those days was for the minister to baptise a child at the parents' house rather than in the church on a Sunday which is more usual now. Margaret Shankland also took me to see the present Monigaff Parish Church which sits in a very prominent position above the village. The church was designed by the architect, William Burn, and built between 1834 and 1836 but in the grounds are the ruins of a much older church building, parts of which are medieval. The Rev. Michael Johnstone was born in Berwick-on-Tweed on 14 May 1811, the son of the Rev. Thomas Johnstone and Lilias, the only child of Rear-Admiral John McKerlie. In its day, the manse at Monigaff must have been a hive of activity as the couple had twelve children, six girls and six boys, several of whom became ministers. Rev. Michael Johnstone was particularly well thought of by his parishioners and apparently was not afraid of innovative ideas, being instrumental in introducing the first organ in the district to his church in 1873. In the present church, where the organ is still in use, there is a plaque to his memory and also a framed photograph, and his tomb is in the church yard near the medieval ruin.

Having discovered so much detail about the birthplace of Joseph William Wilson, it was reassuring to have it all confirmed in the 1881 census. Set against the known information, there are few people who would maintain that there are no human stories behind the official forms. The 1881 census was taken on the night of 3 and 4 April and the entry for the Wilson family is as follows:

PARISH OR DISTRICT, Minnigaff:

CITY OR COUNTY, Kirkcudbright

Wood of Cree Cottage, house with four rooms with one or more windows.

Thomas Wilson, head of family, married, age 45, shepherd, born Barr, Ayrshire

Annie Wilson, wife, married, age 35, born Minnigaff, Kirkcudbright

Thomas Wilson, son, age 8, scholar, born Minnigaff, Kirkcudbright

John McG, son, age 7, scholar, born Minnigaff, Kirkcudbright

James, son, age 5, scholar, born Minnigaff, Kirkcudbright

Margt McW, daugh, age 3, born Minnigaff, Kirkcudbright

Joseph W, son, age 1, born Minnigaff, Kirkcudbright

At this point in my research I was content to conclude the section on

Minnigaff, having gathered what I thought was sufficient information to give a flavour of the Wilsons' involvement at Creewood. I was also conscious of the fact that I had other locations to explore. However, in the time that I had been putting my script together, Robert Horne had been scouring every nook and cranny at Drannandow in the hope of locating the lintel stone from Creewood Cottage. He contacted me early in May 2003 to say that the stone had been found and that if I wished to have it, it would probably fit in the back of my car. For the previous decade or more the stone had lain on the stable floor covered by some loose planks of wood which had formed a dry and comparatively warm bed for Robert's dogs. I travelled to Drannandow a few days later to assess the logistics of moving the stone and returned on 29 May 2003 when Jimmy McEwan and David Ferguson kindly lifted the stone into the back of my car. After lunch with Jean and Robert Horne I set off down the farm road and stopped for a few moments of quiet reflection at the site of what had been Creewood Cottage. I drove more slowly than usual on my way back to Edinburgh as the weight of the stone definitely affected braking distances. At the time of writing, the Creewood stone adorns a small patio in my back garden, awaiting a more permanent resting place.

The carved stone from Creewood Cottage, Minnigaff, was saved when the cottage was demolished in 1967. For many years it lay at Drannandow Farm steadings before being taken to Edinburgh in 2003. *Photograph by Douglas Gould.*

THE LOCHTON CONNECTION

This part of my research began with one word, 'Lochton', which appeared on the birth certificate of Annie Wilson, a younger sister of Joseph. Annie was born at 10.00 pm on 30 April 1883 at Lochton, and her father, Thomas Wilson, informed the registrar, David Millar, at Barrhill on 10 May. But for that single birth certificate, this part of Joseph's life could have been completely overlooked. It is likely that the Wilsons were at Lochton shepherd's cottage, which belonged to the Craigen's Farm, sometime between either August or November 1881, when they left Creewood, and June 1885 when one of the Wilson children was enrolled at New Luce school.

Unfortunately my search of public records for the Wilsons at Lochton was not nearly as fruitful as with other locations. Between August 1881 and June 1885 there was no national census, which deprived me of checking what is usually one of the best sources for finding an entire family. Even worse, I noted that in the census for 1891 and 1901, Annie's birthplace of Lochton did not seem to be confirmed. The 1891 census, which lists the Wilsons at Balmurrie, New Luce, states that Annie was born at Colmonell, and the 1901 census, which lists the Wilsons at Cairnholy, Kirkcudbrightshire, also gives Annie's place of birth as Colmonell. Lochton and Colmonell are both in Ayrshire, about ten miles apart, but whereas Lochton has only a few buildings, Colmonell is a good-sized village. I was more than relieved to be told that Colmonell was also the name of the parish and that there was, therefore, no conflict between the two official sources as the census would be referring to the parish and not the village.

Nevertheless, I was keen to trace some other official confirmation. The Valuation Rolls between 1881 and 1885 made various mentions of Lochton and the neighbouring farms of Lochend and Knockycoid but the occupants of some of the smaller houses were not listed. At one time there was a rule that properties with an annual rent of less than £4 per year were not included. It is very likely that Lochton shepherd's cottage came within that exclusion. I was unable to trace any relevant church records or school admission registers for Barrhill which is the nearest village to Lochton. A good description of Barrhill, covering the period when the Wilsons were at Lochton, appears in Groome's *Ordnance Gazetteer of Scotland* which gives some idea of the services available in the neighbouring village:

> BARRHILL, a village and registration district of Colmonell parish, Ayrshire. The village stands on the river Dusk [now Duisk], 12 ½ miles SSE of Girvan station. Of modern origin, it has a post office, with money order and savings bank departments, a Free church, cattle fairs on the Thursday before fourth Friday of April, August and October, and a lamb and sheep fair on the Thursday before the fourth Friday of August; a public school with accommodation for 200 children, had (1891) an average attendance of 81, and a grant of £74, 6s, 6d. Pop. of district (1881) 1059, (1891) 912.

In more modern times, up until the 1970s, cattle sales were also held on the first Saturday in May and June and on various Saturdays in the autumn.

In fact, confirmation that the Wilsons were at Lochton was held within the family. Mrs Nancy Gardiner, a niece of Joseph William Wilson, recalled being told of the Wilson connection at Lochton when she worked at the neighbouring farm of Knockycoid. She was employed principally as a housemaid, but also worked on the land because of the shortage of male employees during the Second World War. Nancy remembers being at Knockycoid from about 1941 until she got married in 1944. At that time Knockycoid was farmed by the Hyslop family. She remembers that Lochton shepherd's cottage, where her father and his brothers and sisters lived, could be seen from the kitchen window of Knockycoid farm house.

The Cameron family lived at Lochton shepherd's cottage and, nearby, Lochton Mill was still operating.

By this time in my research I thought it was time that I visited Lochton. After spending the previous night at the Stables Guesthouse in Newton Stewart, I took the B7027 through Knowe and past Loch Dornal until I reached Lochton Mill on the east (or right-hand) side of the main road. Like most of the locations where Joseph lived in his early years, Lochton is a very tranquil setting, remote from large centres of population. I had already been told to find Gib Cuthbertson who has lived at Lochton Mill for many years. When I explained the reason for my call, Gib invited me in and gave me a conducted tour of the outbuildings and also the old mill which lay about two hundred yards from his cottage on lower ground near to the Duisk Water. The building had not been used for milling for many years but the layout was still evident and the bulk of the stonework was intact. Although all the mill machinery and most of the wheel had been removed many years ago, there were numerous mill stones scattered around. Gib showed me the raised ground level where the lade had brought the water in, and also the outline of the mill pond which contributed to the head of water needed to drive the mill wheel. Further upstream a natural bend in the Duisk Water marked the spot where the lade water was taken off.

After seeing round the mill, Gib pointed out the position of what had been Lochton shepherd's cottage, now reduced to a pile of stones. The cottage had been set into the side of a hillock a few hundred yards south-west of the mill. I went over to investigate but a profuse crop of nettles prevented me from seeing as much as I would have liked. It was obvious that the cottage had been built to get some protection from the hill but it was not possible to discern which was the front and which was the back. The garden area, perched on the highest part of the ground, was the easiest to locate as it was still marked out by the base stones of an old dry-stane dyke. Further exploration of the site would need to wait for another time, but, before leaving Gib, I had the opportunity to see his collection of walking sticks of every size and style which he had made in his workshop over the years.

Later I drove the short distance to Barrhill where I was to meet Mrs Gaff who had lived at Lochton shepherd's cottage with her husband, son and two daughters between 1945 and 1951. Mrs Gaff remembered particularly the practical difficulties of raising a young family in a small cottage with none of the basic amenities which are now taken for granted. Like the cottage at Creewood, the house at Lochton had no gas or electricity, no running water and only a dry toilet. Water for drinking and cooking was taken from a shallow well some distance from the house. When the Gaff family were at Lochton, it was usually the task of the men folk to carry the water in pails to the kitchen. In the winter the water in the well froze and the surface ice needed to be broken up with an axe, but in the summer, although the level dropped, it did not run dry. Water for cleaning and washing was usually taken from the barrel which collected rainwater from the roof. The house was heated by burning either coal or peat in an open fire in the main room and lighting was by paraffin lamps or Tilley lamps.

At a later date I also had the opportunity of discussing the layout of the cottage with Mrs Gaff's son, John, who is a boat builder and had a clear understanding of the construction of the house. Built into the side of the hill, it was effectively a two-storey building at the back looking north-west, and a one-storey building at the front, looking south-east. At the back of the house, the cobbled ground floor, reached through a wide timber door, was used for sheltering and feeding cattle in the winter. The front of the cottage had a small timber porch protecting the front door. Internally, the short hall gave access to: the kitchen and wash room on the left; a bedroom straight ahead; and the living-room on the right. The living-room was the largest room with a fireplace and oven on the gable wall and a bedbox fitted into the back wall of the house. For the Gaff family the accommodation was fairly limited but for the Wilson family, sixty years earlier, it must have been exceedingly homely. When Annie was born there on 30 April 1883 she had five older brothers and one older sister: Thomas, 10; John, 9; James, 7; Margaret, 5; Joseph, 3; and Robert, nearly 2. Despite the cramped conditions in the house, the Wilson boys must have had a wonderful time playing and fishing in the Duisk Water and watching and helping the miller, John McCutcheon, going about his daily tasks. For small boys in the 1880s there would be no end of interest watching the flow of water, the grinding wheel, the creaking machinery, the dust and the endless visitors coming in with horses and carts laden with sacks of corn and oats for milling.

I cannot be sure when the Wilsons left Lochton but subsequent research shows the family at Balmurrie, New Luce in 1885.

BALMURRIE, NEW LUCE

Before I embarked on the story of my grandfather, I had only a vague idea that he had, at one time, lived in the vicinity of New Luce. Over the years I had visited the village once or twice but I did not know it well, nor had I any knowledge of the surrounding countryside or farms. A few years ago, however, there was a small incident which, in retrospect, might have been an omen. In 1998 when my wife and I were on holiday, living in a remote cottage at Dirnow, west of Newton Stewart, I decided to go for a walk on a unclassified road which ran northwards from Dirnow. It began with forest plantations on either side, and continued into open moorland where there were standing stones on higher ground to the west. The lambing season was well under way and the hillside was full of ewes with lambs only a few days old. When I stopped for a rest on an outcrop of rock above a small loch on the right-hand side of the road, I was aware of a lamb standing bleating some distance from the flock. I watched it for a few minutes by which time a ewe had also separated herself from the group and was looking in the direction of the stray lamb. I have no knowledge of how ewes and lambs behave but it seemed to me that bonding was not taking place as the lamb made no effort to suckle and the ewe looked thoroughly uninterested in what I took to be her offspring. After a moment or two I decided, rather self-consciously (even although the nearest person was about three miles away!) to shoo the lamb gently towards its mother. The idea seemed to work, but only for a moment, and soon the bleating started again and mother continued to show little interest in the lamb, and even less in me. I came to the conclusion that I was not cut out to be a shepherd. Knowing

The external appearance of the buildings shown in this photograph of New Luce, around 1930, had probably not changed all that much since Joseph William Wilson left the village to come to Edinburgh in 1900. New Luce Parish Church, with the small belfry, is in the centre of the picture. To the right of the church is the churchyard, and to the right again, hidden by the trees, is the school. The small building in front of the church was the original school. On the extreme right is the gable end of the Police Station. The two cottages on the left, with the people standing outside, were demolished around 1966 for the construction of one new house. *Courtesy of Neale McQuistin.*

what I know now about the neighbourhood, the incident occurred on the east side of Artfield Fell, only a mile or two from Balmurrie shepherd's cottage where Joseph and his brothers and sisters lived with their mother and father, Annie and Thomas Wilson. Had Thomas or any of the family witnessed my efforts with the lamb they would surely have recommended either further training or an alternative vocation.

In April 2003 I spent a short time in New Luce armed with three pieces of information about Joseph William Wilson. Firstly, I knew from birth certificates that when the Wilsons came to Balmurrie, New Luce, the family consisted of mother, father, Thomas (junior), John, James, Margaret, Joseph, Robert and Annie. The younger siblings, William and Agnes, were born at Balmurrie in 1886 and 1888 respectively. Secondly, I recalled that William Wilson of Kirkmabreck, near Creetown, had told me many years ago that when his brother, Joseph, (my grandfather) had left school, his first job was to work on the minister's glebe at New Luce. Thirdly, I knew that immediately before Joseph had applied to join the Edinburgh City Police in 1900, he had been employed as a farm servant by Mr and Mrs McQuistin of Balneil, New Luce. Whilst the three pieces of information were interesting, they were hardly sufficient to make a story. In fact I made several visits to New Luce before my research was anywhere near to completion.

On arrival in New Luce, I parked my car beside the public hall intending to look round the village on foot. I spoke to Mrs Brooks who was in her garden nearby and discovered that whilst she had been born and bred in the village, she had also lived for a while in Edinburgh within a mile or so of my own house. Mrs Brooks' garden in New Luce backed onto the minister's glebe where Joseph had worked more than a century earlier, and in the distance, the handsome two-storey white building had been the manse, now occupied as a private house. The road up to the manse also led to Balmurrie but that would need to wait for another day as I was already well past the time when I said I would be at the Stables guesthouse in Newton Stewart. Before leaving New Luce, however, I located the village school (now a guesthouse) and Balneil road end where the McQuistins had employed Joseph in 1899. A picture was emerging but I needed to follow up specific leads at a later date.

From my initial visit to New Luce it was obvious that I had the nucleus of a story but I needed to do some serious research to trace whatever documentation was extant. The most likely sources were:

1. the log books and Admissions and Withdrawal Register for the local school;
2. the census returns for 1891;
3. the Valuation Rolls for the 1880s and 1890s.

I discovered that, rather remarkably, the Admissions and Withdrawals Register for New Luce Public School, 1857–1925, had survived and was available for consultation at the Ewart Public Library in Dumfries. Like many similar school records, the 'admissions' part of the register recorded the serial number, name, date of birth, residence, occupation of the parents and date of admission of each pupil. There were additional columns which would have provided interesting information but unfortunately they had not been completed. The columns which had not been completed were headed: whether eligible to Grant; last presented under Standard; date of leaving; time at school; and (perhaps most interesting of all) conduct. Despite these limitations, the school register was an excellent source of information as it confirmed the Wilsons' existence at Balmurrie from at least June 1885.

| (1) | (2) | (3) | (4) | (5) | (6) | (7) |
NO.	NAME	AGE NEXT BIRTHDAY	RESIDENCE	OCCUPATION OF PARENTS	DATE OF ADMISSION	AGE
583	James Wilson	10.10 1875	Balmurrie	Shepherd	June 1885	9
584	Maggie Wilson	10.7.1877	Balmurrie	Shepherd	June 1885	7
596	John Wilson	7.3.1874	Balmurrie	Shepherd	Oct. 1885	11
675	Joseph Wilson	18.6. 1879	Balmurrie	No entry	Oct. 1888	9
687	Robert Wilson	7.5.1881	Balmurrie	Shepherd	Aug. 1889	8
737	Annie Wilson	30. 4. 1883	Balmurrie	Shepherd	Mar. 1891	7
821	William Wilson	1.1. 1886	Balmurrie	Shepherd	May 1894	8
902	Agnes Wilson	8.9. 1888	Balmurrie	No entry	April 1897	8

The eldest sibling, Thomas (born 12 August 1872) is not listed at all. He would have been 13 in 1885 and may well have left school. Joseph was admitted in October 1888 by which time he was 9 and had been at Balmurrie for more than three years. Although the third column in the register is clearly headed 'age next birthday', the headmaster has consistently used the column to record each child's date of birth. For reference, I have added a seventh column to show age on admission, which is not in the register. It is interesting to note that Robert, Annie, William and Agnes were not admitted to New Luce school until they were 7 or 8.

At least eight of the nine Wilson children attended New Luce Public School sometime between 1885 and 1897. I did not, of course, expect to discover eight sets of school report cards completed in every detail, but the information which has survived is sufficient to get some idea of how the school was organised and what was seen as important by the staff and, to some degree, the children. Perhaps more than anything else, it should be remembered that Balmurrie shepherd's cottage was about three miles from the village school. On wet or snowy days, Annie Wilson would have had

Balmurrie shepherd's cottage at Balmurrie Farm in 2003 when it was being used to store farm machinery. The Wilsons (mother, father and nine children) lived there from 1885 until around 1897.

no option but to keep her children at home rather than have them walking for more than an hour in the open countryside. On other occasions, when the weather deteriorated later in the day, Annie would have had the unenviable task of getting half a dozen children's shoes and clothes dried off and ready for school the next morning.

Archival material on New Luce Public School from at least 1857 is available in the Ewart Library, Dumfries. The Admissions and Withdrawals Register, already referred to, confirms that the principal teacher was Robert Calvert Lupton who was in the post until he retired in October 1900. He was assisted by a female teacher, the incumbent, for reasons not recorded, usually remaining in the post for a very short time only. There were also two female pupil teachers who stayed the course for much longer i.e. four or five years. Mr Lupton's salary in 1889, payable quarterly, was £122 per annum, with the free use of a house and garden. By contrast, the vacant post of assistant teacher at New Luce was advertised in 1886 in *The Scotsman* and the *Wigtownshire Free Press* at £40 per annum. Miss Bella Fergusson was appointed out of fourteen applicants but she remained for only six weeks. The school also employed a cleaner, Mrs McGowan, whose wage is not recorded, except that she was given an increase of 6d (2½p) per week 'on condition that the water closets are washed out once a week or oftener if required'. The euphoria of the moment must have died when she was told that the extra 6d was not to be given 'when the fires are stopped'. The water closets were for the use of the staff only; dry toilets were provided for the children. The Board's attitude to the use of the school building for 'extra curricular activities' does not appear to have been consistent. In 1895, Mr Heron, a teacher of dancing, was initially refused permission to hold a dance class in the evening, but permission was granted in the following year to use the school for a Curlers' Ball. In general, however, the Board appeared satisfied with the way the school was run by Mr Lupton: '1884, the school continues to be very carefully taught and good progress on the whole has been made during the past year. 50 pupils presented for Examination.' When Mr Lupton came to retire in 1900 after many years' service, the School Board Minute Book records that there was a minor dispute over the amount of his pension. He declined the first offer of £60 per annum but accepted an increase to £65, 'plus the Government Pension'. Surprisingly, there is no mention of any special event or presentation for

Mr Lupton to mark his long period of service. When Mr Lupton retired on £65 per annum, Joseph was earning £66 per annum in the Edinburgh police.

In 1887, by which time James, Maggie and John Wilson were attending the school, the log books were written up on a daily basis by Robert Jannet described as 'Correspondent'. A few entries give a different angle on the reasons for truancy: '9.2.1887, Nearly all the boys in this department and several in the other absent without leave at the Ploughing Match'; then '22.6.1887, Very few in attendance owing to the demand for turnip thinners.'

My second source of information for the Wilsons at Balmurrie was the census return completed on the night of 5 April 1891. It confirms that they were living at Balmurrie shepherd's cottage, described as a house with three rooms with one or more windows. The head of the household is given as Thomas Wilson, aged 55, shepherd, and his wife Annie, aged 45. Seven of the nine siblings are mentioned: John, 17; Maggie, 13; Joseph, 11; Robert, 9; Annie, 7; William, 5; and Agnes Davidson, 2. The eldest sibling, Thomas Wilson, junior, who would have been 18 at the time of the census, is not mentioned, nor is James who would have been 15. A further search of the census revealed that Thomas Wilson, junior, was listed at Shennanton, Kirkcowan, employed as a shepherd in the household of Alexander McKie, and, in the same census, James is listed at Dilhabboch (now Dalhabboch) near the northern boundary of Inch Parish, in the household of Alexander Rowan, farmer. No occupation appears against James' name. The Valuation Rolls for Shennanton and Dilhabboch around 1891 do not list either Thomas or James as occupiers, which suggests that their accommodation was in the main farmhouses. It seems likely, therefore, that when Thomas and James were old enough to live away from the family home, they took jobs on farms nearby, giving a bit more space for their siblings back at Balmurrie.

The 1891 census also confirms that Balmurrie farm house was occupied by Jessie McMillan, a widow, who had a general servant, Agnes Wilson, and a farm servant, James Murray. To complicate matters, there was a separate two-roomed house listed under the title 'Balmurrie Farm House', which was occupied by another Wilson family. The head of the household was also named Thomas Wilson, aged 57, an agricultural labourer, living with his wife, Ellen Marion; and their son, John, aged 19; daughter, Ellen, aged 23; and two nieces, Jane Wilson, 12, and Jane Agnew, 11.

The third possible source of information was the Valuation Rolls for the time that the Wilsons were at Balmurrie shepherd's cottage, i.e. from 1885. Valuation Rolls are, of course, a very useful source of information but they were never intended to be used for finding one's grandfather. The Lands Valuation (Scotland) Act 1854 established a uniform valuation of land and houses in Scotland. The record lists the names of the owner, tenant and occupier of every house and piece of land in Scotland, with the rather unfortunate exemption (from a genealogist's point of view) that properties in rural areas with an annual value of less than £4 per year did not always include the name of the occupiers. However, from about 1885 another column appears in the Rolls headed 'Inhabitant Occupier' which is very informative. From the 1885–86 Roll, the name Thomas Wilson, shepherd, is listed at Balmurrie and continues until 1896–97 after which a James Murdoch is listed as a shepherd at Balmurrie. This suggests that by 1897 the Wilsons had moved to Cairnholy, Kirkcudbrightshire, probably only a few months after Agnes had started school at New Luce in April of that year.

Having established conclusively that the Wilsons were at Balmurrie shepherd's cottage from 1885 until around 1897 I thought it was time to look at the area in more detail. In September 2003 I spent a couple of days at New Luce. The most obvious base for bed and breakfast was Tha Butchach run by Mr and Mrs Tuckfield in the old school building, which dates from 1865. After the school closed in 1977, the building lay empty until 1985 when it was converted into a care home. The Tuckfield family bought it in 1987 and continued to run it as a care home until September 2002 when they set up the present bed and breakfast establishment.

From New Luce I took the single-track road to Balmurrie farm house where Mrs Elinor McIlwrick and her sons, Gilbert and Ian, kindly showed me round the house and garden. The McIlwricks have farmed at Balmurrie since 1900, a matter of three years after the Wilsons left Balmurrie for Cairnholy. Even after more than a century, the Wilsons' association with the farm is still remembered in two interesting ways. On the outside of the stable door, the McIlwricks have carefully preserved what looks like a small horseshoe but is, in fact, a heel shod from a boot at one time worn by one of the Wilson boys. There is no way of knowing whose boot it came from as all the brothers would have had similar protective pieces fitted to their working boots. In those days, young lads were adept at striking the heel of their boot against a rock to create a momentary spark. For all we know they may well have used the rock which is closely associated with the following anecdote. A few hundred yards towards New Luce there is a large, boulder on the left-hand side of the road which became an important landmark on the journey to school. When the Wilson boys were of school age, one of them acquired the habit of smoking an old clay pipe. Knowing that smoking was forbidden by his parents and the schoolmaster, the young Wilson boy (after having a 'fly puff') would hide the pipe under the big stone and check that it was still there on his way back from school. The story goes that as soon as he was old enough to leave school he stopped smoking! I do know that most of Joseph's adult life he was an ardent pipe smoker, but discovered from Jean Stewart (née Wilson) that the smoker was, in fact, one of my grandfather's brothers – John, or Jeck, as he was usually known. Apparently, much later in life, when Jeck was giving one of his frequent lectures to the Young Farmers' Club at the Waverley Hall in

The smoker's stone at Balmurrie Farm where John McGowan Wilson (Jeck) hid his pipe and tobacco on the way to school. Photographed in 2003.

Creetown, he alluded to the Balmurrie stone with the comment that after leaving school, 'I gave up smoking and started my education.'

Having seen round Balmurrie farm house and steadings, I walked the short distance to the shepherd's cottage where the Wilsons had lived. The cottage lay only a few yards from what is now part of the Southern Upland Way, a concept completely unheard of in the 1880s. The front and back doors were bricked up as were the windows, making it difficult to discern, from the outside, the size of each apartment. The chimneys and the original slated or thatched roof had been replaced by corrugated iron. Internally, the dividing walls had been removed and one end of the cottage had part of the wall taken down to allow access to store farm machinery. When I peeked in to see the internal layout I was startled by two beautiful white barn owls which flew past me to safety. At the opposite end of the house to the open gable was a small stone lean-to outhouse with a cobbled floor, probably used in the Wilsons' time as a byre. Although the front doorway is bricked up, the original, very worn doorstep made a comfortable seat from which I was able to look out over the garden and down the valley towards New Luce. To a city dweller, the silence was breathtaking. For some people it is

The author's notebook lying on the doorstep at the bricked-up doorway of Balmurrie shepherd's cottage where Joseph and his brothers and sisters would have played in the late 1880s. Photographed in 2003.

The original manse building for New Luce Parish Church was extended many years ago by the addition of the two-storey wing to the left of the picture. For several years now the building has been a private house owned by the Buckoke family. Photographed in 2003.

impossible to visit a place like Balmurrie (or Creewood or Lochton), to see where their forebears came from, without being overwhelmed by a feeling of affinity with the location. Sitting in the sun on the doorstep of the house in which my grandfather, Joseph, played and fought with his brothers and sisters, was a very levelling experience. It was a pity when the peace and tranquillity were shattered by the sound of a low-flying fighter aircraft passing immediately overhead.

After leaving Balmurrie and driving back to New Luce I took the opportunity of calling in to the former manse. The house, enlarged many years ago by the addition of a new wing, has been in the private ownership of the Buckoke family almost since it ceased to be a manse. The manse originally stood in policies of several acres which included pasture, a walled vegetable garden and an interesting old stable block which had unfortunately been severely damaged by fire some years ago and replaced by a modern garage. Joseph Wilson had worked on the glebe when he first left school, probably around the year 1893 when he was 14. At that time the minister was the Rev. William Forsyth who had three sons and four daughters born between 1870 and 1882. In recent years, the Buckoke family have undertaken the removal and investigation of the midden which had accumulated over the years at the back of the house on the steep embankment to the Cross Water below. Among the hoard of discarded household items were many bottles, some of them used for medicine and some for medicinal purposes.

My research did not reveal how long Joseph worked on the glebe, nor whether he lived in a bothy at the manse or walked from Balmurrie each day. When his father and mother and some of his brothers and sisters left Balmurrie in 1897 for Cairnholy, Joseph did not go with them. Either he remained at the manse or had moved to Balneil where he was employed as a farm servant immediately before going to Edinburgh at the end of 1899.

While I was at New Luce it was important for me to visit Balneil Farm. I remembered that when I was at a very early stage in my research I had read a reference to the McQuistins of Balneil on Joseph's application form to join the Edinburgh City Police. At the time, I contacted John Wilson of Kirkmabreck Farm who advised me that the McQuistins were still at Balneil. Later, I arranged to see Gordon McQuistin at Balneil Farm where he showed me round the house and steadings. Gordon told me that his family had farmed at Balneil from before 1900 and that it would have been his grandparents, James and Jane McQuistin, who employed Joseph. He knew that the Wilsons had been at Balmurrie and was well aware of the story of the Wilson boy who hid his clay pipe under the big stone. During my visit to Balneil, Gordon showed me the cottage which at one time had been two separate dwellings used by the farm labourers. Almost certainly Joseph lived in some part of that cottage. Unfortunately, no documentary evidence has survived of the McQuistins' occupancy of Balneil prior to 1900 but an informal account book kept by Gordon's father, Andrew, for the neighbouring farm of Barshangan from 1915 to 1920, makes interesting reading. By 1915 Joseph had been in the Edinburgh City Police for fifteen years but the references in the account book give some idea of the life being led by farm servants, some of whom Joseph would have known in earlier years.

The account book allocates a separate page to each employee and gives

the amount of their wages, reduced by various deductions during the course of employment. In 1915 Matilda Wallace was engaged as a housemaid from Martinmas (Scottish Quarter Day 11 November) to May term, at £10. There are various deductions shown: 4th March (Weekend) £1; 21 April (Fair) 10/-; with the balance apparently paid at the end of the period of employment. The deductions from William Gilmour's wages as a ploughman of thirty years' service suggest that he had a wife and family to feed: 15 pounds of butter at one shilling per pound; cheese (amount unspecified) at 9/2d; 10 stones of Indian Meal at 16/-; and insurance at 8/8d. Other deductions, extracted randomly from the account book, include: picnic cash 5/-; 1 cockerel 3/-; razor 5/-; toothache 5/-; Kirk money 2/-; gun licence and cartridges 18/-; tobacco 2/6d; Glenluce dance 10/-. Some employees were hired on a seasonal basis: J. McWilliam was hired on 29 December 1918 'to sned turnips at three farthings per 100 yards. 2/- per day for food'. His contract was concluded with the single word 'gone'. In 1919 James McGibbney was engaged 'for harvest work at £7 (breakfast at home) wife to lift at 5/- per day, dinner and supper'. Also in 1919, Charles Milligan was 'engaged for byres and dairy and to learn cheesemaking, wages £18 per 6 months'. By comparison, in 1914 Joseph was earning nearly £2 per week as a police constable in Edinburgh which had risen to £5 per week as a sergeant in 1920.

Andrew McQuistin's account book was also used to record brief details of the animals' breeding programme: 4 July 1916, Nell mare served by Knockiebay horse; Lady served on 19th June; 1917 Lady served on 4 June with Premier Baron.

My final act at New Luce was to walk the distance from New Luce to Balmurrie shepherd's cottage to get some idea of how difficult (or easy) it was for children to attend school on a daily basis or for Joseph to walk to his work at the minister's glebe or at Balneil Farm. The distance in all three cases is about three miles, in substantially the same direction. I had the

OPPOSITE. James McQuistin and his wife, Mary Jane McQuistin (née Mitchell) photographed at Balneil Farm, New Luce, on the day of their Golden Wedding anniversary on 22 September 1930. The family celebrations were held in the barn at Balneil. Mr and Mrs McQuistin employed Joseph William Wilson as a farm servant immediately before he joined the Edinburgh City Police in 1900. Mary Jane McQuistin died, aged 82, on 20 January 1939, and James died, aged 86, a few weeks later on 22 March 1939. *Courtesy of Gordon McQuistin, grandson of James and Mary Jane McQuistin.*

Balneil farm house, New Luce, in 1930. Left to right: Muriel McQuistin, aged 7; Bob McGuire; Winnie McQuistin, aged 6; and Tom McQuistin. On the left of the picture is the hand water-pump which was in use when Joseph William Wilson lived and worked at Balneil.
Courtesy of Mrs Winnie Adams, née McQuistin.

A moment's respite during harvesting at Mains of Larg, New Luce, in the 1920s, with John Forster driving the horse-drawn reaper. Joseph William Wilson would have been familiar with the scene and probably knew the families involved, even although he had left the district several years earlier.
Courtesy of Nigel Forster, grandson of John Forster.

distinct advantage of doing the walk on a beautiful autumn evening with no wind and no rain. From New Luce the road rises fairly steeply past the manse and what was known as 'Kelly's Spoot', which provided clear spring water from a small outcrop of rock on the right-hand side of the road. About a mile further on, the road flattens out and begins to rise again where Balmurrie comes into view. The valley of the Cross Water lies to the left, beyond which are the farms of Barshangan and Knockiebay. Over the last half mile of the walk, the road again becomes quite steep, particularly as it passes the boulder where Jeck Wilson hid his pipe. By then I, too, was puffing. Shortly after, I reached Balmurrie shepherd's cottage slightly more than one hour from starting my walk. On the return journey it was beginning to get dark but there was a good moon which was much more apparent (and useful) than if I had been walking on a city street. The deathly quiet was interrupted only occasionally by the bleating of a lost lamb, or the slightly louder sound of water running in the numerous small burns feeding the Cross Water below. By the time I was passing the old manse it was completely dark, the lights of the upper windows visible over the boundary wall. Joseph would have recognised the scene – except perhaps the electric light and the car in the driveway.

The Wilson family left Balmurrie shepherd's cottage, probably towards the end of 1897. By then the oldest sibling, Thomas, was 25 and the youngest, Agnes, was 9. Joseph was 18 and was either working at the manse or at Balneil. We also know that at the time of the 1891 census, Thomas and James had already left home. It is clear, therefore, that the family had begun to disperse when Thomas and Annie moved to Cairnholy, Kirkcudbright-shire.

THE KAIN FAMILY AT DUMFRIES

Having discovered a little about the early life of my grandfather, Joseph William Wilson, I then turned my attention to finding out more about the family background of my grandmother. I knew that she had a rather long name, Mary Jane Mathieson Kain, that she had had a great regard for her younger brother, John, who died during the First World War, and that she probably came from Selkirk. At an early stage in my research I discovered that Mary Jane had, in fact, been born in Dumfries on 5 June 1883. Subsequent research into the family became so difficult and confusing that I required the assistance of a professional genealogist, Jean Moore, to unravel some of the problems. I was also hampered by the fact that, unlike the Wilson side of the story, where numerous relatives had helped with information, I was not able to find any members of the Kain family.

Archibald Kain, a grain dealer from Irongray, near Dumfries, married Elizabeth Taylor sometime prior to 1855 when the registration of marriages became compulsory. No record has been found of their date of marriage. They had several children, one of whom was Jane Kain my grandmother's mother. As Jane Kain's full date of birth has not been established, it is not possible to give her exact age at given times. To make matters worse, her age is not always given accurately on various forms: usually it varies by a year or two.

Jane Kain, my grandmother's mother, was born at Irongray, probably in 1854, before the compulsory registration of births was introduced in 1855. She spent her early years in Dumfries up until around 1889. To say that Jane had a difficult life is something of a understatement. Her early adult years were blighted by poverty, the lack of a father figure in the household, illness, child disability, early mortality and a sense of general hopelessness, eased from time to time by Poor Relief and the support and assistance of neighbours and friends.

On 22 November 1872 when Jane was about 18 years of age and unmarried, she gave birth at Troqueer to a daughter, Janet, whose birth certificate states that she was illegitimate. It also states that Jane was employed as a kitchen maid. After some initial dispute, the father was named as William Thomson. On 17 December 1875, Jane gave birth at a house in Two Closes, High Street, Dumfries to her second child, a son, Wellwood, whose birth certificate says he was illegitimate and does not provide details of the father, or the parents' marriage. Wellwood appears to have been born with both mental and physical disabilities. At the time, Jane was employed as a domestic servant. On 7 July 1877 when Jane was still unmarried she gave birth to her third child at No. 55 Loreburn Street, Dumfries: a son, John, whose birth certificate says he was illegitimate and does not give details of the father. Jane's occupation is again given as domestic servant. On 27 May 1879 young John died at No. 9 Chapel Street, Dumfries, his mother's residence at the time being given as 'S. Counties Asylum, Dumfries'. The primary cause of John's death is given as bronchitis and the secondary cause, rather surprisingly, as teething. My immediate assumption was that Jane Kain, worn out by the trauma of single-handedly looking after three children, had been admitted to the asylum at the age of 25.

The Southern Counties Asylum, Dumfries (now demolished) was the second house for psychiatric patients on the site of Crichton Royal Hospital. The reference, on the death certificate, to the asylum, was so integral to the story that I enlisted the help of Mrs Morag Williams, the Dumfries and Galloway Health Board archivist who kindly searched all the indexes of admissions around 1879, revealing that Jane Kain had not, in fact, been admitted as a patient. Mrs Williams thought that the most likely explanation was that Jane had been employed at the hospital and was

OVERLEAF. A muzzled bear with its keeper in the High Street, Dumfries, *c.* 1900, watched by a large group of children, some apprehensive, some curious and some full of misplaced confidence. The Hole i' the Wa' Inn, with the ornamental lions at first floor level, is still an important hostelry in Dumfries. *Courtesy of Dumfries and Galloway Council Libraries, Information and Archives.*

required to 'live in' at the staff accommodation. Apparently, providing staff accommodation was closely linked to better attendance figures, particularly where the hospital was remote from where most of the staff lived. The death certificate for John Kain states that he died, aged 22 months, at 6.30 am on 27 May 1879, and that it was Jane Kain herself who registered the death at Dumfries on the same day. Unfortunately I did not discover where young John was buried. The death was certified by Dr William Carruthers of Dumfries, who was probably Jane Kain's family doctor, although the concept of a 'family doctor' would not then be quite so well defined as it is today. He also held the position (usually in rotation for one year only) of house surgeon and apothecary to Dumfries and Galloway Royal Infirmary but he died very young, at age 23, in April 1882.

Mrs Williams' intuition was rewarded when she made a further search of the hospital records and located details of Jane Kain's employment. According to the Southern Counties Asylum monthly pay lists to 1 December 1879, Jane Kain was employed as an attendant at a yearly wage of £16, with the sum of 1/6d deducted for her uniform. As her monthly pay was £1: 5 : 2d, it appears that the deduction of 1/6d for the uniform was made *every* month. Jane started work at the hospital shortly before December 1878 and appears to have left in January 1880. In 1879, when Jane was working and living at the hospital, she had already had three children: Janet, 7; Wellwood, 4; and John who had died that year. There is no information on who looked after the children when Jane was at the hospital. It is likely that they were cared for at No. 9 Chapel Street, but as the Valuation Rolls for 1879 to 1880 gave details of several tenants at No. 9, there was no way, at that stage in my research, of identifying which family was involved.

In addition to Jane Kain's employment record, the General Rules for the Guidance of the Attendants have survived for the year 1873 from which it is clear that a high standard of patient care was expected:

> RULE 3 Under no circumstances shall any Attendant in charge of Patients ... leave or lose sight of the Patient without handing over the charge to another Attendant.

> RULE 4 No attendant is permitted on any account to strike any Patient, or push, or pull him about.

RULE 7 dealt at length with the management of the Patients with separate categories under the headings: a) Cleanliness and Dress; b) The Distribution of Food at Meal Times; c) Exercise in the Open Air; d) Occupation and Amusement; e) General Quietness and Good Conduct; f) Attention to the Patients in regard to the Calls of Nature.

Mrs Williams also traced entries in the 1880 Minute Book of Dumfries and Galloway Royal Infirmary, which was, of course, an adjacent, but completely separate, hospital to the Southern Counties Asylum. The minutes for the Weekly Committee refer to a Jane Kain being admitted on 26 April 1880, on the recommendation of Dr Kerr, and being dismissed (or discharged) on 17 May 1880. No case notes have survived to ascertain the reason for admission or the treatment given. The same Minute Book also refers to a Janet Thomson Cain being admitted on the recommendation of Dr Thomson on 15 June 1880 and again on 12 July, before being discharged on 19 July 1880. Again there are no surviving case notes and the name of the patient gives cause for speculation. Our Janet (born on 22 November 1872) has 'Kain' on her birth certificate but the spelling 'Cain' has appeared in other documents. No previous record has been found of our Jane having a middle name 'Thomson' but it will be recalled that Janet's 'disputed' father was named on the birth certificate as William Thomson.

The 1881 census, taken on 4 April 1881, places Jane Kain at No. 38 North Queensberry Street, Dumfries, living in a one-roomed house with her 8-year-old daughter, Janet. Her son John is obviously not listed as he died in 1879. Wellwood would have been 5 years of age and should have been listed but he is not. A further search, by Jean Moore, of the 1881 census traced a most interesting entry which tended to confirm that Jane Kain needed a lot of assistance in caring for her children. Thomas Wilson, a 61 year-old labourer and his half-sister, Rachel Easton, aged 70, were living in a two-roomed house at No. 9 Chapel Street, where young John had died two years earlier. Living with Thomas and Rachel was 'Nellwood Cain',

OVERLEAF. Surviving records show that Jane Kain was employed as a resident attendant at the Southern Counties' Asylum from around December 1879 to January 1880 at an annual wage of £16, from which the sum of one shilling and sixpence was deducted each month for her uniform. *Courtesy of Dumfries and Galloway Health Board Archives.*

No.	NAME.	Employed as.	Date of Entering Service.	Yearly Wage.	
32	Eliz.ᵗʰ Mc Naught	Attendant	Nov 1878	14	„
33	Jane Kain	do.	Dec 1878	16	„
34	Janet Thomson	do.	Feb. 1879	15	„
35	Eliz.ᵗʰ Murray	do	Ab 1840	15	

No.	NAME.	Employed as.	Date of Entering Service.	Yearly Wage.	
28	Joan Kirkpatric	do	Dep 1877	14	„
29	Harriet Rae	do.	Dep 1877	14	„
30	Eliz.ᵗʰ Mc Naught	do.	Nov 1878	14	„
31	Jane Kain	do.	Dec 1878	16	„
32	Janet Thomson	do.	Feb 1879	15	
33	Eliz.ᵗʰ Murray				

1st Decr. 1879

Deducted on account of.	Amount Deducted.	Advance of Wages for Good Service.		Yearly Advance Retarded on account of.	Amount Paid.		
		Date.	Amount.				
Brought Forward £					71	4	1
Uniform	1/6				1	6	10
do.	1/6				1	5	2
do.	1/6				1	3	6
do.	1/6				1	3	6

1st January 1880

Deducted on account of.	Amount Deducted.	Advance of Wages for Good Service.		Yearly Advance Retarded on account of.	Amount Paid.		
		Date.	Amount.				
do.	1/6				1	6	10
do.	1/6				1	6	10
do.	1/6				1	6	10
do.	1/6	(Left)			1	4	8
do.	1/6				1	3	6
do.	1/6				1	3	6

ABOVE. The Female Sitting-Room at the Southern Counties' Asylum, Dumfries where Jane Kain was employed as a resident attendant. This undated photograph shows two of the staff in a sitting-room in the enlarged north, or female, half of the building.
Courtesy of Dumfries and Galloway Health Board Archives.

LEFT. A beautifully ornate staircase in the Southern Counties' Asylum where Jane Kain was employed as a resident attendant. Her duties would also have included cleaning and polishing – including the balustrade.
Courtesy of Dumfries and Galloway Health Board Archives.

aged 5, born in Dumfries, and classified in the census as disabled. Despite the variation in the name, it is beyond doubt that the entry refers to our Wellwood. The name 'Nellwood' instead of 'Wellwood' is obviously a transcript error, and, as already observed, the family name 'Kain' was frequently given as 'Cain'. The entry not only confirms that Wellwood was informally adopted but indicates that he was severely disabled.

On 5 June 1883, when Jane was about 29 years of age and unmarried, she gave birth, at Spur Inn Close, South Queensberry Street, Dumfries, to her fourth child, Mary Jane Mathieson Kain (my grandmother) who was also illegitimate. Jane's occupation is given as 'sewer in woollen mill' but again there are no details of the father. At the present day, the family still recall that our grandmother was given her very long-winded name from a neighbouring family (in Dumfries?) who were kind to Jane Kain after she gave birth to her fourth illegitimate child. The 1881 census, as we have seen, places Jane Kain at No. 38 North Queensberry Street and just next door, at No. 40, was an unmarried lady called Mary Mathieson, a provision dealer or grocer, who was living with her niece, also Mary Mathieson, another niece, Jane Mathieson, a sister Janet, and a 13-year-old boy, James M. Armstrong. Sometimes it can take a long time to get to the source of a rumour.

On 9 July 1887, when Jane was about 33 and unmarried she gave birth to her fifth child, a son, at No. 13 Friar's Vennel, Dumfries. The birth certificate says he was illegitimate and does not disclose the name of the father. Jane named her second son, John, after the son of the same name who died in 1879. At the time her occupation was given as domestic servant.

No further family has been traced but in the following year, on 24 August 1888, Jane's first child, Janet, died of kidney disease at No. 12 Irish Street, Dumfries at the very early age of 15. The death certificate gives Jane's occupation as 'formerly general servant'. The certificate also has an amendment in Column 1 in answer to 'Rank or Profession'. The word 'Invalid' has been inserted, then deleted, and replaced with the word 'Single', followed by 'Illegitimate'. Young Janet was laid to rest in St Michael's Cemetery in Dumfries on Tuesday 28 August 1888. The extract from the burial register says that she was buried at a depth of 7 feet in lair 30 of Section X. Initially, the register referred to lair 4 in the Free Section

but this was altered, and the appropriate payment made i.e. 4/6d for the lair and 15/- for the interment fee. Presumably Jane managed to find the money (equivalent to about three-quarters of her monthly wage at the hospital in 1879) to avoid committing her child to a pauper's grave. The lair also contains, at a depth of 6 feet, the body of Violet C. McHolme who died at No. 12 Irish Street aged 1 year and 8 months on 7 January 1889, and was buried on 9 January. No headstone has been erected for either child. The only obvious connection between the two burials is the address, No. 12 Irish Street, where both children died. Jane Kain and Violet's mother, also Jane, were obviously neighbours, probably of about the same age and living in a similar domestic environment. It seems likely that the two mothers came to some kind of arrangement to share the lair. Jane Kain would only be too aware of the trauma of a young death in the family.

The town of Dumfries was so integral to the Kain family story that I thought more information must be available. Unfortunately, I was not able to trace any of Jane Kain's offspring attending school even although Janet, Wellwood and probably Mary Jane would have been of school age at the time. That is not to say that they did not attend school, it is simply that the Admissions Registers have not survived: the most likely school was Loreburn St John's in Newall Terrace. I also checked the relevant years of the Register of Boys in Dumfries Industrial School 1881–1922. The register contains a short history of each of the boys admitted, many of whom had family backgrounds similar to the Kains, but there was no record of either Wellwood or John (the second) being admitted. Equally disappointing was my failure to locate any references to the Kains in the very extensive indexing of local newspapers held at Ewart Library. There were, however, many references to the Kains in the Poorhouse minutes which I was able to consult at the Dumfries and Galloway Archive Centre in Burns Street, Dumfries. It is interesting to link these references with Jane Kain's known circumstances, gleaned from other sources.

OPPOSITE. The Three Crowns Inn or Hotel in Three Crowns Close, which ran between Loreburn Street and Queensberry Street, Dumfries (1885). Mary Jane Mathieson Kain was born in the adjacent entry, Spur Inn Close, on 5 June 1883. She would have been familiar with this scene and probably knew some of the people in the photograph. The Three Crowns Inn was the principal building in the close but the 1887 *Report on the Dumfries Closes* (referred to in the text) indicates that the smaller dwellings were not in nearly such good condition.
Courtesy of Dumfries and Galloway Council Libraries, Information and Archives.

The notebook shows the position of Janet Kain's unmarked grave, lair 30 of Section X in St Michael's Cemetery, Dumfries. Janet died, aged 15 years, on 24 August 1888, and was buried on 28 August.

Dumfries had two Poorhouses. One was Rosevale House in the Cresswell area, founded in 1854, which became a maternity hospital in 1939. The other was at Moorheads in St Michael's Street, built in 1753 at the expense of two brothers, merchants from Dumfries, James and William Moorheads. In Moorheads' Minute Book for 1888 there is a long list of rules and regulations, a breach of which was sufficient to classify an inmate as 'disorderly'. The rules included anyone who: 'makes any noise when silence is ordered to be kept; does not daily cleanse his person; or behaves improperly at public worship or at prayers'. The punishment imposed by the Governor included either extra work or 'withholding all milk or butter milk which such inmate would otherwise receive with his meals'. With an obvious eye for future technology, one of the working committees recommended to the Board on 20 December 1888 to have the office and Poorhouse connected to the telephone system 'seeing that the cost for both connections would only be £14 per annum'.

The Poorhouse minutes include the name, but not the address, of the many people who were either admitted as inmates or qualified for some form of Poor Relief. The indexes include the name 'Jane Kane' and 'Janet Kane' but the actual references appear to confuse the two individuals, and there is the usual variation in the spelling of the surname. Sometimes the minute shows that an entire family was admitted. It is unclear from the Jane Kain references whether she alone was admitted, or whether her children were also admitted. Either way, the entire family was in receipt of Poor Relief, probably in the form of food provision, for many years.

The earliest references to Jane Kain in the Poorhouse, that I could find, are 4 June 1875 and 13 September 1883 which say: 'Jane Kane – Relief continued – claim on Irongray'. The reference to Irongray suggests that the Poorhouse was reimbursed by the Parish of Irongray where Jane was born in 1854. The use of the word 'continued' also suggests that Jane had been given relief before 1875 but I was not able to trace this. In 1883 Jane was living at Spur Inn Close and had just given birth to my grandmother, Mary Jane. The next reference is dated 31 December 1885 when Jane Kane appears under the list of Pauper Cases in receipt of Relief. By 11 March 1886 her circumstances had deteriorated further and she was admitted to the Poorhouse as an inmate, but, again, it is not clear if her children were also taken in. In 1886 Jane was still living at Spur Inn Close and had three surviving children: Janet, 14; Wellwood, 11, not resident with her; and Mary Jane, 4. Throughout 1886 Jane had various spells of being given Relief and being admitted, and was later admitted on 20 September 1888. The most poignant reference, however, is dated 4 October 1888 when Jane Kane 'applied for and was granted education to Mary Jane, 5 years and 3 months'. Other than her birth certificate, this is the earliest official record that I have traced of my grandmother, Mary Jane Mathieson Kain. In 1888 local public schools, run by School Boards, charged fees, depending on the age of the child, and Jane Kain could obviously not afford to pay. The last reference in the Poorhouse records that I could trace for Jane was dated 21 February 1889 when she was re-admitted, shortly after the death of her daughter, Janet. Ironically, at the time of this admission, Jane had been living at No. 92 St Michael's Street, almost opposite the Poorhouse. By moving across the road to a much bigger house she had come up in the world: it was clean and tidy; the meals were regular and wholesome; and it even had a telephone!

At this stage in my research I felt that I had discovered a fair amount about my grandmother's family and the various addresses at which they had lived. All the indications were that the Kains lived in very modest accommodation but I still did not have much information on their actual living conditions. This gap in my research was comprehensively filled when the staff at the Archive Centre in Burns Street referred me to the *Dumfries Closes, 1887*, an official report on the condition of the buildings and washing and sanitary facilities in the principal closes. The report was of particular relevance to my study as it included Spur Inn Close, Friar's Vennel and Irish Street where the Kains had lived in the years around 1887. It should be remembered that the poor state of some houses in Dumfries, at the time of the report, was no different from that in many other towns throughout Scotland. The report begins with a general description of each close and the condition and cleanliness of the buildings. It then goes on to tabulate: the number of separate families; the number of apartments; the number of occupants; and the number of children under 5 years of age. The second part of the report deals with the provision of water closets, sinks and drainage, and the last part lists the improvements which needed to be made. The report is too lengthy to reproduce here but the following excerpts give a flavour of how basic life was for the Kains and many other similar families.

Spur Inn Close, No. 6 North Queensberry Street, Dumfries where Mary Jane was born on 5 June 1883: sometimes Spur Inn Close was described as in North Queensberry Street and sometimes in South. The two streets were later renamed Queensberry Street, presumably to avoid the confusion. The close is described as open and airy, about twenty feet wide, with cobbles, mostly in good repair but broken at the gullies or gutters. In total there were 64 occupants, 6 of whom were under 5 years of age (17 families), living in 32 apartments, having the use of 4 water closets (3 outside and 1 inside) and 5 sinks. Many of the fittings were defective and in one case, described in the report as 'an objectionable arrangement', there was a tap in the lobby which had no sink at all and only a bell trap in the floor to take away the waste water. As the report does not include the names of the occupants, it is not possible to identify which apartment was used by the Kains. Some were obviously worse than others.

No. 13 Friar's Vennel (North side) where John Kain (the second) was born on 9 July 1887, the year in which the report was written: the general description of the close says it was 'fairly clean' and 'newly white washed': perhaps the walls were whitewashed but the remainder of the report certainly wasn't. In total there were 54 occupants of whom 11 were under 5 years (14 families), living in 24 apartments, served by very inferior sanitary arrangements. There were 3 water closets, one of which was out of order. One of the functioning water closets was shared by 43 occupants, 7 of whom were under 5 years. Not surprisingly, this water closet was described as being in a very dirty state. Even worse, several tenants did not even have a key to the door. The provision of sinks was equally bad. Only one dwelling was fitted with a sink, the other tenants having to use 'gullies and watertaps in the Close'. Sometimes, in the winter, they would be frozen up, and at all times of year there would be a total lack of privacy.

No. 12 Irish Street where the Kains lived in 1888: again the general description 'fairly clean' does not give any great cause for concern. However, of the three addresses relevant to the Kains, this is unquestionably the most unhygienic. There were 114 occupants, 19 of whom were under 5 years of age (23 families), living in 53 apartments. The report says: 'The most densely populated place yet met with'. The situation regarding the water closets beggars belief by modern standards, with 1 water closet for 21 occupants; 1 water closet for 44 occupants; 2 water closets for 49 occupants; and 1 water closet 'out of use through the empty trap of which sewage gas escapes'. By contrast, there appears to have been a good provision of sinks and the additional 'refinement' of a slop trough and a water fountain in the close. On 24 August 1888, the year after the report was written, Jane Kain's first child, Janet, died of kidney failure, aged 15, somewhere in this wretched environment.

Jane Kain was in Dumfries from at least 1872, when Janet was born, to at least 1889 after Janet died. In these seventeen years the family can be traced at, at least, nine different addresses. Five illegitimate children were born, two of whom, John (the first) and Janet, died before adulthood. It seems likely that Jane Kain decided to leave Dumfries shortly after the death of Janet on 24 August 1888. The last reference to Jane in the Poorhouse minutes is 22 February 1889. By the time of the 1891 census Jane Kain was in Hawick with her daughter, Mary Jane Mathieson, and her son, the second John. My suspicion that Wellwood had been left behind in Dumfries was confirmed by a curious entry in the 1891 census. Thomas Wilson, who had been helping to look after Wellwood at No. 9 Chapel Street at the time of the 1881 census, had died in 1890 leaving his half-sister, Rachel Easton, to care for Wellwood on her own. The census places Rachel in a two-roomed house at No. 50 North Queensberry Street where she is described as the head of the household, aged 80 and employed as a charwoman. Wellwood is also listed, described as a boarder, aged 14, occupation, scholar. At the time of the census he would actually have been 15. That entry seemed to complete the story – except for one small detail. In the 1891 census, Wellwood's surname is given as 'Kirk' and not 'Kain' or 'Cain'. Presumably, or perhaps hopefully, the error has occurred owing to some misunderstanding between Rachel Easton, who was quite elderly, and the census enumerator. At the present day, the computerised indexing of the census information is a wonderful tool but, understandably, was hard-pressed to find 'Kain' under the 'Kirks'.

Wellwood probably remained with Rachel Easton until her death in 1895 after which another neighbouring family, by the name of Goldie, appear to have taken over his care. One of the Goldie family, George, employed as a newsboy, was about the same age as Wellwood and almost certainly assisted him in taking on the same occupation. Wellwood had many health problems, of course, but managed to attend school and also hold a job as a newsboy. Sadly he died at 8.00 pm on 11 April 1898 at No. 81 Loreburn Street, Dumfries. On his death certificate his age is given as 20 but, in fact, he would have been 22, and his occupation is given as newsagent. No information at all is given in answer to the question asking for details of the deceased's father and mother. The cause of death is given as Angular Curvature of the Spine, Asthma and Bronchitis and the death certificate is signed by Hugh Cunningham, MD. The death was reported

Section _2_ No _97_ Price £ /·5/

GRANT OF RIGHT OF BURIAL		BURIALS
Name of Purchaser	Name of Deceased	Wellwood Kane.
George Goldie.	Occupation	newsagent.
Occupation	Place of Death	81 Loreburn St.
newsagent.	Date of Burial	14 April 1898.
Residence	Age	20 years.
81 Loreburn Street	Depth of Grave	7 feet.
Date of Purchase		
13. April 1898.		

The notebook shows the position of Wellwood Kain's unmarked grave, lair 97 of Section Q in St Michael's Cemetery, Dumfries. Wellwood died on 11 April 1898 and was buried on 14 April. His death certificate says he was 20 but he was, in fact, 22.

to the Dumfries Registrar on 13 April 1898 by George Goldie. Attached to 'Qualification of informant and residence if out of the house in which the death occurred' there is a single word 'Occupier'. As the Valuation Rolls for 1898 list George Goldie at No. 81 Loreburn Street, it is reasonable to assume that Wellwood was living with, or near to, the Goldie family when he died.

George Goldie was born in 1874 at No. 5 Union Street, Dumfries. In 1881 he was at No. 35 Loreburn Street, in 1891 he was at No. 50 North Queensberry Street, and in 1901 he was at No. 167 High Street. All these addresses are near to where Jane Kain was living but we have no way of knowing what contact, if any, there was between Wellwood and his mother and siblings. Wellwood was buried in lair 97 of Section Q in St Michael's Cemetery, not far from his sister Janet's grave, on 14 April 1898. The lair was purchased for £1, not by his mother as I had hoped, but by George Goldie, newsagent, No. 81 Loreburn Street, Dumfries. It is obvious that George Goldie took a very active role in looking after the interests of Wellwood Kain. When I visited St Michael's Cemetery on 16 June 2004 the cemetery staff assisted in locating the position of the grave. There was no headstone but I did wonder if Jane had travelled to the funeral from Selkirk where she was living in 1898.

During the course of my research I visited Dumfries on several occasions in an endeavour to locate one or other of the many houses in which Jane Kain and her family resided. More than a century of redevelopment, however, has changed the environment substantially from the days of Jane Kain. Two Closes, where Wellwood was born in 1875, was on the

High Street, Dumfries, looking north-west towards the Burns' Monument and Greyfriars' Church, 1906, with Chapel Street on the right.

This existing building, Nos. 13 and 15 Friar's Vennel (on the left) photographed *c.* 1935, is believed to date from the early eighteenth century. Jane Kain and her family were resident at No.13 when John (the second) was born in 1887. No. 13 was reached from the small doorway to the left of the man with the cap. The building was divided into several one-roomed apartments when the Kains were living there. *Courtesy of Dumfries and Galloway Libraries Information and Archives.*

south side of the High Street between Crown Close and Royal Oak Close. The site of it is near the present-day branch of Littlewoods on the High Street. I also visited Loreburn Street where John (the first) was born in 1877 but I could not locate the house. The site of No. 55 is now occupied by a red sandstone block of houses and shops, with a date stone 1925. Chapel Street runs from the High Street to Queensberry Street, and beyond into an attractive cul-de-sac, but there is no sign of the original No. 9 where John (the first) died in 1879. I also discovered that North Queensberry Street and South Queensberry Street appeared to have been renamed Queensberry Street, and the houses renumbered which made it impossible to trace No. 38 North Queensberry Street where Jane Kain was living at the time of the 1881 census. I had slightly more luck with Spur Inn Close, South Queensberry Street where Mary Jane was born in 1883. Spur Inn Close ran

St Michael's Church, and the domed Burns' Mausoleum on the right, are obviously the main subjects of this picture, *c.* 1860. On the extreme left, however, one of the small houses forming part of St Michael's Street was where Jane Kain lived with her family (at No. 92) before leaving Dumfries in 1889. *Courtesy of Dumfries and Galloway Libraries Information and Archives.*

from South Queensberry Street to Loreburn Street, parallel to Three Crowns Close but was demolished many years ago for a Post Office delivery van depot. No.12 Irish Street, where Janet died in 1888, appears to have disappeared for the construction of a car park and bus depot.

So much then for the Kain family's built heritage: it has all been demolished – except, that is, for one small property. No. 13 Friar's Vennel, where John (the second) was born in 1887, still exists as part of a building which is believed to date from the early nineteenth century. I enquired at No. 15 which is occupied as a gents' hairdressers and was lent the key for the small timber door which led to No. 13 at the rear of the building. I was not able to contact anyone on my first visit but subsequently I met Hugh Campbell, the owner, who believed my story and allowed me to see round the house. In 1887, the household probably consisted of: Jane Kain, aged 33, employed as a domestic servant; her daughter, Janet, aged 15, who was probably in very poor health; Mary Jane, aged 4; and the newly-born son, John (the second). At the present day, the first floor flat consists of four apartments and a bathroom but is much more extensive than it was in 1887. There is a living-room, bathroom and bedroom looking out to Friar's Vennel and a kitchen and second bedroom to the rear of the property. It was an interesting experience visiting No. 13 as it was the only house where the Kains had lived which I had managed to locate. It is interesting to speculate on whether Mary Jane, my grandmother, would have remembered the house. She was just past her fourth birthday when young John was born. Her older sister, Janet, would have lived there but John (the first) died before Mary Jane was born. Mary Jane could have been near her fifth birthday when the family left Friar's Vennel for Irish Street. It is possible, therefore, that Mary Jane would have had a hazy recollection of the house in Friar's Vennel. When the Kains were at Friar's Vennel, Wellwood was living only a few hundred yards away. Even if Mary Jane did not know that Wellwood was her brother, she almost certainly had seen him playing in the neighbouring streets.

I also checked the Valuation Rolls for the town of Dumfries between 1872 and 1902 in the hope of tracking Jane Kain at the addresses already discovered. With the exception of Two Closes, off the High Street, I was able to find a reference to Jane Kain at all the addresses during the years I was expecting. The entries vary between 'Miss' and 'Mrs' and between 'Kain', 'Kane', and 'Cain'. In every case the entry suggests that Jane Kain was living in very modest accommodation as the rental value for her house or apartment was always either the lowest, or among the lowest, in the building. Frequently the relevant addresses are listed as 'lodgings'. The Valuation Rolls also revealed a further address for Jane Kain which does not feature on any census form, birth certificate or death certificate for the family. The 1889–90 Valuation Roll lists Jane Kain paying a rent of £3: 18/- at No. 92 St Michael's Street, Dumfries. That section of St Michael's Street was demolished many years ago and is now grassed over, but its proximity to the historic St Michael's Church has ensured its place in history. A surviving picture of St Michael's, *c.* 1860, includes a short row of houses, one of which is No. 92. This was the last house in Dumfries occupied by Jane Kain and her family before they moved to Hawick.

THE KAIN FAMILY AT
HAWICK AND SELKIRK

Jane Kain and her family moved to Hawick probably in 1889. The first official confirmation is in the 1891 census which places Jane in a one-roomed house at No. 10 Wilton Crescent, with her daughter, Mary Jane, aged 7, and her son, John (the second) aged 3. There is, of course, no mention of Wellwood, who would have been 15, as he had been left behind in Dumfries. In 1891, Wilton Crescent was populated mainly by men and women who worked in the local woollen mills. Wilton Public School was nearby where both Mary Jane and her younger brother, John, attended. It is not known if they also attended Wilton Parish Church which was beside the school off Princes Street.

On 13 July 1894 Jane Kain married Alexander Mair when they were both living at No. 5 Round Close, High Street, Hawick. According to the marriage certificate he was a 43-year-old bachelor, employed as a wool sorter and she was a 39-year-old spinster, employed as a wool factory worker – who had already given birth to five children. The common thread, which bound them together, was obviously the textile industry, but we do not know if she pulled the wool over his eyes or if it was he who spun the first yarn. Either way, their hearts were entwined and – better late than never – my great-granny tied the knot.

Having established the two addresses in Hawick where Jane Mair (Kain) lived with her husband (and presumably Mary Jane and John), I decided to see if the actual houses still existed. I was heartened to discover that Wilton Crescent was shown on a modern map of Hawick but when I

The High Street, Hawick, showing the tower and clock of the Town Hall completed in 1887. Round Close runs north-west from the High Street, near the light-coloured car parked on the left. *From* The Story of Hawick *by W. S. Robson, first published in 1937.*

got there I found that the houses looked as though they had been built in the 1970s. Clearly Jane Kain's house had been demolished. I had better luck at Round Close, however, which is on the north side of the High Street, slightly to the west of Hawick's magnificent baronial-style Town Hall. Several houses in Round Close were still standing but many others had been demolished and it was not possible to say where No. 5 had been. However, I had a remarkable piece of luck when I contacted David Hill of Hawick Museum. He was able to produce a photograph of Round Close showing two female neighbours chatting at the door of one of the houses. Unfortunately there was no way of establishing their identity. There were also several photographs of Wilton Crescent, *c.*1966, shortly before the old

houses were demolished. One of the photographs, taken from the air, was easily aligned with the 1964 Ordnance Survey map which included house numbers. The position of No. 10 Wilton Crescent on the aerial view could then be located and compared with the land pictures of the street in 1966. No. 10 appears in one of the photographs to the left of the only car in the street. It was part of a row of terraced houses with a window on either side of a central doorway and two small dormers in the roof space. When Jane Kain was there in 1891, No. 10 was divided into several very small apartments.

The demolition of the Wilton district was obviously keenly felt, and lamented, by many Hawick residents, particularly David Hill, the writer and poet, whose poem describes the desecration in the colourful language of the Hawick vernacular. His words are reproduced here by courtesy of his son, also David Hill:

GABLE-END

I watched the deliberate
Last Destruction o Wulton
Yin simmer Setterday efternune
Wulton was biggit in comely stane
Quarried frae native hills –
Frei-stane and whun ...

And I saw a bull-dozer
Bashin at a fower-fit gable
O' whun. Bashin. And gaun back.
And bashin. And aye the whun,
Wi mortar mixed wi Te'iot grevel –
Sma, sma stanes; a study their-sel –
Aye the whun stude: dour shoodert,
Waitin for the next daud ...

OPPOSITE. Jane Kain married Alexander Mair at No. 5 Round Close, Hawick, on 13 July 1894. The buildings shown in the picture have all been demolished but probably included No. 5. The date of the photograph and the identity of the two ladies are, unfortunately, unknown. *From* The Story of Hawick *by W. S. Robson, first published in 1937.*

Wilton Crescent, Hawick, *c.* 1966, shortly before it was demolished. Jane Kain and her family, Mary Jane and John (the second) lived at No. 10 at the time of the 1891 census. At that time the property was probably divided into small one-roomed apartments. The door to No. 10 is on the left, opposite the refuse bucket nearest to the Mini. *Courtesy of Hawick Museum, Scottish Borders Council.*

And there cam to my mind,
Watchin this odds on duel
Wi a machine that was bund
To wun i' the end, the thocht
O' auld mason-tredsmen
Lang-syne deid, that built,
And built weel wi this thrawn stane
Sae like their-sels – mebbe watchin,
And allowi' this fecht
Atween their creative hard-work
And a destructive stinkin deevil,
And cheerin on that auld gable-end –
The Last Wulton Resistance –
Cheerin like hell! But kennin.

Aa went away, wae,
For auld crafts and lost skills
Afore it cam daudin doon.

Jane and Alexander Mair left Hawick shortly after they were married, probably in 1895, and moved to Selkirk.

There is no magic formula for tracking people's changes of address which occurred more than a hundred years ago but trial and error usually produce some kind of result. On the plus side I knew that my grandmother, Mary Jane, had let it be known in the family that she had come from Selkirk. Although she was not born in Selkirk, she certainly lived there for several years.

Selkirk Library has an excellent collection of archival and local history material at St Mary's Mill in Level Crossing Road. Having already discovered that they had several Admissions Registers for the local schools, covering the period of the 1890s, I decided to give them a call. The first register was for Selkirk Burgh School in Chapel Street from 1874 to 1909. The index had an entry 'Mary Jane Kain, 1083'. On locating reference 1083 the following information was obtained:

DATE OF ADMISSION: 13.8.1895
NAME: Mary Jane Kane
NAME OF PARENT OR GUARDIAN: Jane Mair
ADDRESS: 10 Dunsdale Haugh
WHETHER EXEMPTION FROM RELIGIOUS INSTRUCTION
IS CLAIMED: No
DATE OF BIRTH: 5.6.83
LAST SCHOOL (IF ANY) WHICH CHILD ATTENDED
BEFORE ENTERING THIS SCHOOL: Wilton P. S., Hawick
DATE OF LEAVING: left blank

In local history, or family research, an entry of this nature is like gold dust. The entries are so authentic and not usually capable of being misinterpreted. Despite the different spellings of 'Kain' and 'Kane', it is beyond doubt that the entry refers to Mary Jane Mathieson Kain who would have been 12 years of age at the time. It also provides the date when Jane Mair

(Kain) probably came to Selkirk; it gives the home address; and it even confirms that Mary Jane had previously been at Wilton Public School in Hawick.

I had also hoped that the Admissions Registers would have included Mary Jane's younger brother, John (the second) who would have been 8 years of age. Unfortunately it did not. I tried the Admissions Registers for the other schools but again without result. I had put all the registers together ready to return to the librarian when I thought that I would have one final trawl through the whole lot. The first one I picked up was for Knowepark School between 1890 and 1899. It fell open at the Js and there, at the bottom of the page, was 'John Kain, 686 and Mary Kain 694'. Approximately 110 years ago the headmaster had inserted the two Kain siblings as a footnote on the J-page because the K-page was already full. How unthinking of him: he should have known that I might have missed it! Reference 686 for John Kain provided the following information:

DATE OF ADMISSION: 6.8.95
NAME: John Kain
PARENT OR GUARDIAN: Mrs Kain
ADDRESS: 10 Dunsdalehaugh
D.O.B. 10 7 87
LAST SCHOOL: Wilton, Hawick
DATE OF LEAVING: left blank

Again the entry refers, beyond doubt, to John Kain, younger brother of Mary Jane. The entry refers to Mrs Kain whereas it should have been Mrs Mair and John's date of birth is given as 10 July whereas it should have been 9 July.

It seemed to me unusual that the two children, Mary Jane, aged 12 and John, aged 8 should attend different schools when they were both living at the same address. Dunsdalehaugh was in the low-lying north end of Selkirk near all the mills and Knowepark School was, and still is, in Curror Street. The distance from Dunsdalehaugh to Knowepark School is much shorter than the distance from Dunsdalehaugh to Selkirk Burgh School in Chapel Street. The entry for Mary Jane, wrongly indexed under the Js, is interesting. It reads: '694, Mary Kain' but the only column on the page

The building on the left, with the tall chimney, is the Tollhouse, Ettrick Terrace, Selkirk, *c.* 1960. In the mid-1890s, Mary Jane and her younger brother, John (the second) would pass the Tollhouse each day when walking to school from their house at Dunsdalehaugh.
Courtesy of Robert D. Clapperton Photographic Trust.

This 2004 photograph shows the top end of Ettrick Terrace, Selkirk. The blocked up wall is about the position of No. 7 where Jane Mair (Kain) lived with her husband, Alexander Mair, and her son, John (the second) in 1901.

which has been completed is headed 'Cause of leaving', and the entry is 'left the same day'. The entry is not dated but the previous entry, No. 693, is on 7. 8. 95. The most likely explanation is that Jane Mair (Kain) enrolled both Mary Jane and John at the nearest school, Knowepark, but for reasons not now known Mary Jane did not remain at Knowepark and was transferred to Selkirk Burgh School one week later. Perhaps she had a tantrum!

Around 1898-99 Jane Mair (Kain) and her husband, Alexander, moved from No. 10 Dunsdalehaugh to No. 7 Ettrick Terrace, which lay between the Fleece Hotel and the War Memorial, and appears to have been owned by a Miss Elizabeth Brown and let to at least four families, all of whom worked in the mills. Alexander Mair, a wool sorter, is listed in the 1898–99 Valuation Rolls, paying an annual rent of £6. The 1901 census says the property had one room (with at least 1 window) and the residents were:

> Alexander Mair, head, mar., age 50, wool sorter,
>   born Hawick
> Jane Mair, wife, mar., age 47, no occupation, born Irongray
> John Mair, son, unmar., age 13, scholar, born Dumfries

At the time of the 1901 census Mary Jane was nearly 18 and had left home.

After the 1901 Census

The census taken on 31 March 1901 is probably the last official reference to the Mairs as a family. By that time Jane Mair (Kain) was not in employment and was almost certainly not in good health. She died on 24 July 1901 at No. 7 Ettrick Terrace, Selkirk, at the age of 46, the principal cause of death being given as neurasthenia, a form of neurosis. Her husband purchased, in perpetuity, lair 27 in Section I of Brierlaw Cemetery in Selkirk and she was laid to rest at the proverbial depth of six feet on Saturday, 27 July 1901. Unfortunately, when I visited the cemetery in March 2004, I discovered that no headstone had been erected. An epitaph would have been helpful to say the least – or even a wee note about Wellwood!

Shortly after the death of Jane Mair, her widower, Alexander Mair, returned to his home town of Hawick. He was resident at No. 55 High

The small white tag on the grass marks the position of lair 27 Section I of Brierlaw Cemetery in Selkirk where Jane Mair (Kain) was buried on 27 July 1901.

Street, Hawick immediately before his death on 19 December 1908, aged 57, at Hawick Cottage Hospital. When I was researching the burial records for Jane Mair there was no difficulty in finding the cemetery and lair number. I was expecting to find Alexander had been interred in the same plot as his wife – but he was not in any of the Selkirk burial records. The next most obvious place to look was Hawick. The officials who look after the burial records were able to tell me that Alexander Mair was buried at 2.00 pm on 21 December 1908 in lair 5874 of the Burghal section of Wellogate Cemetery in Hawick. It seemed to me a bit of a mystery as to why Alexander was not buried with his wife, Jane, at Selkirk, particularly as he had bought the ground in perpetuity and no other person had been buried in that lair. Initially, it was an even bigger mystery why he was interred in lair 5874 at Wellogate. Mary Storrie and Anthony Boiston Storrie had a child, Mary Watson Storrie, who died aged 6 weeks in December 1903. A. B. Storrie purchased two lairs, 5873 and 5874. His young daughter was interred in 5873, and 5874 was left unused until Alexander Mair died in 1908. That is not all that unusual except that when A. B. Storrie died in 1911, he was interred in 5874 above Alexander. When Mary

Storrie, the widow, died much later, in 1941, she was interred with her daughter in 5873. The situation, therefore, is that 5873 holds the remains of mother and child, and 5874 holds the remains of father, and Alexander Mair. When I visited Wellogate Cemetery in Hawick I discovered that no stone had been erected over either 5873 or 5874. I thought, wrongly, that a bench seat had been erected rather near to the lairs but the cemetery staff measured the ground accurately and confirmed that the bench seat was close to, but not over, either of the lairs. It was comforting to know: it is one thing to share a lair; quite another to share a bench seat. Later research confirmed that Alexander Mair's sister, Margaret, was the mother of Alexander Boiston Storrie. On Alexander Mair's marriage certificate to Jane Kain, one of the witnesses is William Storrie (his brother-in-law) and on Alexander's death certificate the informant is given as 'A. B. Storrie, Nephew'.

By 1908 when Alexander Mair died, the Kain family was greatly depleted: John (the first) had died in 1879; Janet had died in 1888; Wellwood had died in 1898; and Jane Kain or Mair had died in 1901. Only Mary Jane Mathieson Kain and her younger brother John Kain had survived. Mary Jane's life is fully documented in later chapters but John Kain remained something of a mystery.

John Kain

In connection with John Kain, I knew: that he was born on 9 July 1887 at No. 13 Friar's Vennel, Dumfries; that in 1891 he was at No. 10 Wilton Crescent, Hawick, with his mother and sister, Mary Jane; that he was probably at Round Close after his mother got married to Alexander Mair in 1894; and that in 1901 he was at No. 7 Ettrick Terrace, Selkirk with his mother and step-father. After that I lost track of him. In 1901 John was 13 and may well have moved to Hawick with his step-father, who died in 1908. By 1908 John was 21 and presumably had started a career of his own. He had, of course, lost his whole family except his older sister, Mary Jane, who had married in 1904 and was living in Edinburgh. It is possible that John also moved to Edinburgh after the death of his step-father. The present family has always believed that at some time in his life John Kain or Mair served a prison sentence, and that he died during the First World War. Endless searches of prison and court records did not reveal any details of John Kain or Mair and initially almost the same lack of progress was encountered with the military records, but for entirely different reasons.

In the Service Departments Registers at the General Register Office in Edinburgh there is a reference to a Pte. John Kain, Rgtl. No. 40442, Royal Scots Fusiliers, age 38, born Scotland, died in France on 12 October 1916, 'cause of death, dead (presumed)'. Enquiry at the Commonwealth War Graves Commission, the Scottish National War Memorial at Edinburgh Castle, and the National War Museum of Scotland all confirmed the entry for the Royal Scots Fusiliers. That, of course, was not the end of the story, as John Kain or Mair was not 38 when he died: he was 29. In addition to that, there were several other possible entries for Kain, Kane, Cain, Mair or even Moir, if written badly. The problem that I had was that the military records had several feasible entries but none of them had sufficient detail to link them to my John Kain. What I needed was the military record to confirm John Kain's date of birth, exact place of birth or next of kin, but that was not forthcoming. In some desperation I consulted the book *Shot at Dawn* by Julian Putkowski and Julian Sykes which gives an account of the 312 soldiers shot in the First World War by authority of the British Army Act. Thankfully, I found no relevant entries.

The general feeling in the present family was that John Kain died during the First World War, probably as a result of enemy action, but no one could be sure. An interesting item, held by my sister Mary had the potential to resolve the deadlock. This is a brooch or locket which was made from a button from John Kain's uniform. Inside the locket is an early photograph of John's sister, Mary Jane, but there are no other identifying details and no one knows how it came to be in the possession of Mary Jane. Was she given it before John went to war or after he died? Enquiry at the National War Museum of Scotland confirmed that the button was a general service issue and did not, unfortunately, identify the actual regiment.

At this stage in my research I decided to do what I probably should have done right from the start, and that was to engage the services of someone skilled in searching the National Archives at Kew. With the permission of Chris Baker of Great War Family Research I quote excerpts from his very comprehensive report:

ROLL OF INDIVIDUALS entitled to the Victory Medal and/or British V

On 11/11/18 or on becoming non-effective		NAME	Unit previously served with. Regtl. No. and Rank in same on entry into theatre of war	Theatres of war in			
Regtl. No.	Rank			From	To	From	To
40438	A/Cpl	GOODESS David A.	8-R.Scots 8174	Oll	l		
			Pte.				
			2-R.Sc.Fus.				
			11-R.Sc.Fus.				
40442	Pte.	KAIN John	2-R.Sc.Fus. 40442			✓	
			Pte.				
40443	Pte.	KEAN Robert	2-R.Sc.Fus. 40443			✓	
			Pte.				
40444	Pte.	LAMB Stewart	2-R.Sc.Fus. 40444			✓	
			Pte.				
40446	Pte.	MERRILEES Gilbert	2-R.Sc.Fus. 40446			✓	
			Pte.				
40447	Pte.	MIDDLETON Thomas H.	2-R.Sc.Fus. 40447			✓	
			Pte.				

I certify that according to the Official Records the individuals n

Place HAMILTON.

Date 30-6-20.

8—1

This extract from the Medal Entitlement Index confirms that Pte John Kain, Regt No. 40442 of the Royal Scots Fusiliers qualified for the Victory Medal during the First World War. *Crown copyright: National Archives, Kew.*

		Clasps awarded (to be left blank)	Record of disposal of decorations		REMARKS
			(a) Presented (b) Despatched by Post (c) Taken into Stock		
From	To				

...anted under Army Orders **301 & 266** of 1919.

...s ROLL are entitled to the Medal or Medals a...

ABOVE. This extract from the Medal Entitlement Index confirms that Pte John Kain, Regtl No. 40442 of the Royal Scots Fusiliers qualified for the Victory Medal and/or the British War Medal during the First World War. *Crown copyright: National Archives, Kew.*

RIGHT. This is the only known photograph of John Kain, the younger brother of Mary Jane Mathieson Kain or Wilson. John was born on 9 July 1887 at No. 13 Friar's Vennel, Dumfries, and is believed to have died at the Battle of the Somme on 12 October 1916. *Courtesy of Mrs Mary Sneddon, née Cant.*

LEFT. Mary Jane Mathieson Kain or Wilson whose photograph is contained in the button brooch. *Courtesy of Mrs Mary Sneddon, née Cant.*

The brooch made from a button from John Kain's uniform contains a photograph of Mary Jane Mathieson Kain or Wilson. It is not known if she acquired the button before or after John's death in 1916. *Courtesy of Mrs Mary Sneddon, née Cant.*

JOHN KAIN

There are two sources of information about men who died during the war: one, as you are well aware, is the Commonwealth War Graves Commission. A second is *Soldiers Died in the Great War, 1914-19*.

On searching for John Kain in *Soldiers Died*, I discovered only one man by that name – which surprised me. This man had appeared in the CWGC records, but they carried no information that would tie him to 'the' John Kain. The *Soldiers Died* details do, and there is a reasonable prospect that we have identified him.

The soldier in question was 40442 Private John Kain, 2nd Battalion, the Royal Scots Fusiliers. He died on 12 October 1916 on the Somme. According to *Soldiers Died*, this man was born in Dumfries, lived in Edinburgh and enlisted in Glasgow.

His CWGC record is barren of personal information, and this is because when the then Imperial War Graves Commission sent a Final Verification Form to the named next of kin, circa 1920, it was not returned.

I searched too for the Kane and Mair variants, and for all spellings I could think of. However, while there were a considerable number of men by those names, not one had a Dumfries connection. I even searched for men named John who were born in Dumfries – no fewer than 74 men of this description died in the war – but no surnames near to Kain came up, with the exception of the man I have named above.

At my request Chris Baker went on to search that soldier's Service Papers knowing that, unfortunately, a very large number of these were, rather ironically, destroyed as a result of enemy action during the Second World War. Again, quoting from Chris Baker's report dated June 2004:

SOLDIER'S SERVICE PAPERS
The WO363, the 'Burnt Series' of Great War soldiers documents held at the National Archives in Kew, has been thoroughly searched for soldiers matching the description, including the possible name variants Kane and Mair. There are no papers that could be identified as being John's.

Just in case, we also searched the WO364 and PIN26 series, which were unlikely sources as they contain – in theory at least – only papers of men who survived and were discharged to pension. Unsurprisingly, we could find no trace of John there either.

Our conclusion is that the papers no longer exist.

MEDAL ENTITLEMENT DOCUMENTS

We also searched the medal entitlement indexes. Working in conjunction with CWGC records and *Soldiers Died in the Great War 1914-19*, it appears that the only man we initially identified, 40442 Pte John Kain, 2nd Royal Scots Fusiliers, is a reasonable fit to the description if we assume that John Kain did indeed die during his war service. A copy of his documents is attached to this letter.

This John Kain qualified only for the British War Medal and Victory Medal which tells us that he did not cross to France before 1 January 1916.

By examining other sources, we believe that John may not have been in France long before his death in October 1916. No soldier with a regimental number in the 40000 series died before that month. We believe that he would have enlisted in February or March 1916. This timing is interesting, for it means he may have enlisted under the 'Derby Scheme', a voluntary forerunner of conscription.

According to CWGC records, John Kain died on Thursday 12 October 1916, a dull but dry day where the maximum temperature on the Somme battlefield was 61 degrees F. The attack in which John was killed was part of what is now officially known as the Battle of the Transloy Ridges, a phase of the Battle of the Somme 1916.

On the basis of Chris Baker's findings, on a balance of probabilities, John Kain died in action at the Somme on 12 October 1916. I also checked the War Memorials at Dumfries, Hawick, Selkirk and Edinburgh but I was unable to find the name John Kain or Mair.

CAUSEWAYSIDE, EDINBURGH
AND THE CALL OF HOME

Before I embarked on research into the life of my grandfather, I was aware: that he had come from Galloway to Edinburgh to join the police; that he had been attached to Braid Place Police Station; that he had married my grandmother, Mary Jane Mathieson Kain; and that they had raised a family at Braid Place and later at Summerhall Square, before moving to No. 57 Priestfield Road in their retirement. That was about the sum total of my information but by the time I had finished my earlier research I had discovered a fair amount about the early years of Joseph William Wilson and Mary Jane Mathieson Kain. Unlike my research at Creewood, Lochton and New Luce for Joseph, and Dumfries, Hawick and Selkirk for Mary Jane (where I had to find the actual locations), the Edinburgh addresses were already very familiar to me.

Joseph's early years in Edinburgh as a bachelor

At an early stage in my research I was fortunate to trace an Edinburgh City Police document which provided several excellent lines of enquiry. The exact function of the undated form is not clear but it gives the impression that it has been drawn up to bring together historical information about Joseph, up to the date of his death, possibly to confirm his widow's entitlement to a pension. The form provides: the name, Joseph William Wilson; Police Sergeant 96; born 18 June 1879; died 16 January 1958; date of appointment, 2 January 1900; retired 22 September 1930. It also gives his marriage date, 2 June 1904 and the name of his spouse, Mary Kain, who was born on 5 June 1883. Two entries appear opposite 'Children living under 16 years', namely, Joseph, born 10 May 1915 and John, born 27 February 1923. Apparently, the police application form completed by Joseph gave his occupation as Farm Servant, his address as Cairnholy, Creetown, his place of birth as Newton Stewart, and, perhaps most informative of all, his previous employers as Mr and Mrs McQuistin of Balneil, New Luce. I remember when I first saw this reference to the McQuistins of Balneil that I contacted John Wilson, previously of Kirkmabreck Farm, who gave me the McQuistins' telephone number at New Luce, and within five minutes I was speaking to the descendants of the McQuistins who had employed Joseph more than a century ago. Sometimes, Scotland can appear to be a very stable country!

The existence of this initial document led to the discovery of a vast number of other documents, papers and records pertaining to Edinburgh City Police held by the Edinburgh City Archivist at the City Chambers in the High Street. My hope was that they would reveal details of Joseph's police career. Over the course of many weeks I waded through more than 6,000 pages of police information, which at times was interesting, often deadly boring, occasionally humorous and, on one occasion, sufficiently upsetting to put a stop to my research for the day.

According to the *City of Edinburgh Constabulary Police Report* for the year ending 31 December 1900, the total strength of the force was 575, of whom 488 were Constables. Joseph William Wilson was one of them, appointed as PC 761 on 2 January 1900 to C Division as a 'Temporary Constable appointed for cabling Operations'. Exactly what was meant by 'cabling operations' I do not know: in the records there are frequent references to vandalism to cabling, suggesting that it may have been in connection with the cabling system installed in main roads for the cable-car tramway system. C Division included Southside, Abbeyhill, Portobello, Piershill and part of the parish of Duddingston, all under the able command of the Superintendent, James Minty. The total strength was 115 made up of 1 Superintendent, 4 Inspectors, 15 Sergeants and 95 Constables.

Reference to official forms and documents can never provide a full picture of life as a young Constable in Edinburgh City Police in 1900 but the General Order Book does give a flavour of what were seen as important day-to-day guidelines:

> 17.6.1900.
> Lengthy rules about saluting: when the Superintendent enters ... the Police are to stand to attention and the first man who perceives the Chief Constable or Superintendent approach is to give notice to the others by calling out 'attention'.

> 27.7.1900.
> Juveniles should not be placed in cells with drunken and deprived [sic] persons, nor respectable female Prisoners with Prostitutes.

> 9.11.1900.
> Cable tramways – problems with vandalism on the rails and points.

> 9.11.1900.
> Lengthy Regulations introduced for buildings in which billiards and bagatelle is [sic] played.

Most of the information regarding PC 761, Joseph William Wilson, is contained in a series of Weekly Records now held by the Edinburgh City Archivist. The earliest ones were completed by hand by the Superintendent and sent to the Chief Constable's Office. They referred by collar number, name and rank to Admissions, Advancements, Promotions, Commendations, Punishments, Resignations and Retirements, enabling a researcher, with a modicum of patience, to track an individual career. The reference to Punishments was quite illuminating, the offences of insubordination and being under the influence of drink while on duty accounting for the largest proportion. The latter offence attracted a scale of punishments dependent upon the seriousness of the circumstances: at the lowest end of the scale an officer could expect a reprimand and the cancellation of a couple of days' leave, but for serious repeat offences the punishment was instant dismissal, or as the report euphemistically said, the culprit was 'invited to resign'. The Weekly Record did not specify rates of pay but the information could be gleaned from other references e.g. 'P.C. 570 reduced to 28 shillings (£1.40p) for being under the influence of drink when on duty'.

PC 761 Joseph William Wilson was almost certainly attached to Braid Place Station from the outset where he made good progress during the first two years:

2.4.1900 P.C. 761 Joseph W. Wilson From 5th to 4th class
2.10.1900 P.C. 401 Joseph W. Wilson From 4th to 3rd class
1.10.1901 P.C. 401 Joseph W. Wilson from 3rd to 2nd class

No explanation is given for the change of collar number from 761 to 401. However, towards the end of 1902, the Weekly Records included a short report which stopped me in my tracks: it was not that I felt any disappointment at the content; it was simply an overwhelming feeling that I had invaded my grandfather's privacy and that there was no need for me to know what was written there. On the very last page of the 1898–1902 volume is the short report:

26.Dec. 1902
P.C. 401 Joseph Wilson – Two days' monthly leave stopped
for being under the influence of drink on duty and relieved
in consequence.

That is the full extent of the entry, but it was Boxing Day and the incident may well have been the aftermath of an enjoyable Christmas Day. The punishment was at the lowest end of the scale and does not appear to have had any lasting detriment to Joseph's career as he received further advancement on 5 January 1904 'from 2nd to 1st grade 2nd Class'. Some of the punishments meted out to other officers suggest that it was a fairly harsh regime and that the punishment was not always commensurate with the seriousness of the offence. One officer was fined one shilling (5p) for carelessness in signing his name on the pay-bill at the wrong place, the fine being equivalent to about 3% of his weekly wage. A similar fine of one shilling was imposed on PC 628 for an offence which, on the face of it, appeared to be much more serious, assuming, at any rate, that it was the constable who had the blackened eye!

18.7.1900
P.C. 628 Robert Sinclair. Fined one shilling for being drunk while on duty and parading before the Chief Constable with a blackened eye.

It was not all stick, however; occasionally the carrot was produced, for example, when PC 442, Alexander Strachan, was awarded ten shillings (50p) on 26 January 1900 for 'courageous conduct in stopping a runaway horse'.

The police records, unfortunately but understandably, did not provide Joseph's first Edinburgh address but most of the family of my generation remember their parents making references to the family home at Braid Place (now Sciennes House Place) and Summerhall Square. Many of us remember being told that Joseph and his wife Mary Jane lived at Braid Place first and Summerhall Square later, but no one seemed to know where Joseph had lived before he got married. The timing of my research was fortunate as it coincided with the release of the 1901 national census which was taken of all people resident in Scotland on the night of 31 March 1901. Without access to the 1901 census, a significant part of Joseph's early life in Edinburgh would not have been discovered. As expected, Joseph William Wilson is listed. He is one of five people in a two-roomed house at No. 105 Causewayside. He is described as a boarder, single, aged 22, Police Constable, born in Minnigaff, Kirkcudbrightshire. The head of the household is given as Mary Fyfe, a 44-year-old widow living with her 8-year-old son, also Joseph, and her 4-year-old daughter, Annie. There was another boarder, William Russell, single, aged 20, who was also a Police Constable. The names, Mary, Joseph, Annie and William, may well have made Joseph Wilson feel at home, being the same as his own name and that of his future wife, his sister and brother. The remainder of the entries for No. 105 provide a fascinating picture of life in Causewayside at the beginning of the twentieth century. A total of 24 houses is listed, occupied by a total of 128 people, giving an average of 5.3 per house. The smallest number in any one house was two and the largest eight. Some of the larger households contained quite a mixture of relationships which must have put enormous pressure on aspects of privacy and comfort. The various relationships included wife, husband, son, daughter, sister, niece, father-in-law, visitor and boarder. The reference to the houses having only two rooms is in response to: 'Number of rooms with one or more windows'. It follows, therefore, that there could also have been a box room, perhaps let out to boarders. There is no way of being sure, but the sleeping arrangements in Mrs Fyfe's house could have been: living-room, Mrs Fyfe; bedroom, son and daughter; boxroom, two Police Constables – hopefully on opposite shifts! The 1901 census does not give any information on the washing or toilet facilities, but there may have been only communal toilets on each landing or level of the four-storey block. There would certainly have been no fitted baths. By modern standards the houses would be considered grossly overcrowded but it is unlikely to have been a problem for Joseph who was born in a small cottage at Creewood housing eight people, and went on to another small house with more siblings at New Luce.

No. 105 Causewayside is still standing (as at April 2004) and is not in an area destined for immediate redevelopment. It is on the east side of Causewayside almost opposite Grange Court, with a narrow frontage to the main street. Like most Edinburgh stairs nowadays, the outer door is locked but when I visited in April 2003 a lot of renovation work was being done, and, clipboard in hand, I managed to get access without attracting too much attention. There are still 24 flats, presumably with much more modern plumbing throughout. The entire building is laid out in a style unlike most other tenement buildings in Edinburgh. The stairway, with windows on the south side of the building, gives access to the individual flats off a series of iron balconies which provide an airy atmosphere in the summer but are probably very draughty in the winter. I was keen to find out how old the building was when Joseph lived there and what further details could be established. Many of the building plans submitted for approval to Edinburgh's Dean of Guild Court have survived and are available for research but unfortunately the plans for No. 105 could not be traced. Subsequent research has shown that Nos. 99–123 Causewayside were at one time owned by the Royal Association for Incurables, Longmore Hospital, which probably had the tenement built, either as a property investment or to house members of staff. In 1902 at least two of the flats at

The photograph shows Nos 18-26 Causewayside in 1900, the year in which Joseph William Wilson joined the Edinburgh City Police attached to Braid Place Police Station. No. 34 Causewayside, where Joseph was living in 1904 before he got married, forms part of the tenement on the extreme left of the picture. The scene, the shops and the people would have been very familiar to Joseph. *From the Yerbury Collection.*

No. 105 were still occupied by hospital staff. However, in 1897, shortly before Joseph arrived in Edinburgh, Longmore Hospital applied to the Dean of Guild Court to demolish the buildings Nos. 107–123 (leaving No. 105 intact) and to erect on the cleared site a chapel and mortuary. The plans, drawn by the architects Peddie and Washington Browne, of No. 8 Albyn Place, positioned the chapel nearest to Causewayside and the mortuary nearest to the Longmore Hospital. The proposed building allowed for an ice box in the mortuary, a room for post mortems, a photographic dark room and a small museum. When the demolition work was going on, the opportunity was taken to instal an improved water system to the hospital and to widen Causewayside near its junction with

Salisbury Place.

It is not known how long Joseph remained at No.105 but his marriage certificate for 2 June 1904 gives his address as No. 34 Causewayside. The 1901 census for No. 34 shows that there were six separate families with a total number of inhabitants of 37, divided between two, three and four-roomed flats. Clearly, as many of the houses were much bigger, overcrowding was not such a problem as it had been at No. 105. There is no way of knowing which flat at No. 34 was occupied by Joseph in 1904, but the Valuation Rolls for around that time list a Mrs Ann Ferguson, living alone, who might have been Joseph's landlady. No. 34 no longer exists but a photograph survives which shows Nos. 18–26 and the gable wall and two windows of the adjacent tenement which included No. 34. The building was on the west side of Causewayside near the short lane, Sciennes Place, which connects Causewayside to Sciennes. Many of the buildings around No. 34 were demolished years ago when Bertrams, the paper-making machinery engineers, wanted to expand their Sciennes Works. After Bertrams left Sciennes, the site on which No. 34 stood was redeveloped as modern housing.

Joseph William Wilson and Mary Jane Mathieson Kain

Joseph, aged 24, and Mary Jane, aged 20, were married on 2 June 1904 by the Rev. David A. Rollo, minister of Buccleuch Parish Church, which suggests that Joseph and/or Mary Jane were members of that church in Buccleuch Street. Mr Rollo was the minister at Buccleuch from 17 May 1901 to 24 September 1907 when he was translated to Springburn in Glasgow. Joseph and Mary Jane's wedding ceremony, however, was conducted at No. 50 Sciennes in the presence of Robert Wilson and Rachel Cessford. Robert Wilson was presumably Joseph's younger brother, but no information was forthcoming on the identity of Rachel Cessford. The inference was that she was a friend of Mary Jane, in which case she could well have come from outside Edinburgh. The marriage certificate gives Mary Jane's status as spinster and her occupation as domestic servant, residing at The Farm, Dalzell, Motherwell. Several members of the present family recall hearing that Mary Jane had worked for the Duke of Buccleuch

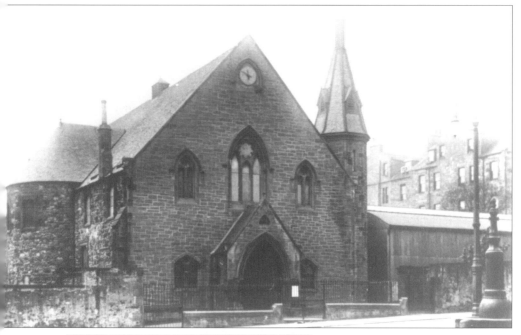

ABOVE. Buccleuch Parish Church in Buccleuch Street as it looked when Joseph William Wilson first came to Edinburgh in 1900.
From the Malcolm Cant Collection.

LEFT. The Rev. D. A. Rollo married Joseph William Wilson and Mary Jane Mathieson Kain at No. 50 Sciennes on 2 June 1904. He was minister of Buccleuch Parish Chuch from 1901 to 1907 and probably also took the burial service for their first child, Tommy, who died on 17 December 1905.
Courtesy of Edinburgh City Libraries and Kirk O' Field Parish Church.

whose family owned Dalzell estate. In view of my previous research into the Kain family, I was rather surprised to note that the marriage certificate listed Mary Jane's parents, both deceased at the date of the marriage, as: father, Alexander Kain, Grocer; mother, Jane Mair, previously Kain, maiden surname Taylor. Joseph's parents, Thomas and Annie Wilson, were both alive at the date of the marriage and living at Cairnholy Farm, near Creetown, but we have no way of knowing if they (or any of the siblings other than Robert) were present at the wedding.

It seemed to me that the information in the marriage certificate suggested at least four separate lines of enquiry:

1. Where and when did Joseph and Mary Jane meet?
2. Who was their bridesmaid Rachel Cessford?
3. Why did Mary Jane's particulars not coincide with my previous research?
4. What was the significance of No. 50 Sciennes?

WHERE AND WHEN DID JOSEPH AND MARY JANE MEET?

I was not aware of where Joseph and Mary Jane first met but there has always been the story in the family – told many times by Mary Jane but usually only to her female grandchildren – that when Joseph first proposed he was told by Mary Jane to go away for a year and if he was still keen at the end of the year, then they would marry. Needless to say the answer to this most human of stories does not repose in New Register House – or at least not in any of the documents that I have looked at!

In the hope of discovering where Mary Jane and Joseph's paths had crossed, I returned to the official records, although the task would have been made much simpler had either of them kept a diary! There are four official sources which help to track Joseph William Wilson and Mary Jane Mathieson Kain: their birth certificates in 1879 and 1883; the 1891 census; the 1901 census; and their marriage certificate in 1904. The obvious starting point was their birth certificates. As we have seen, Mary Jane Mathieson Kain was born at 3.00 am on Tuesday, 5 June 1883 at Spur Inn Close, South Queensberry Street, Dumfries, to Jane Kain, whose occupation was given as 'sewer in woollen mill'. The birth was registered by the mother, Jane Kain, at Dumfries on 25 June 1883. No information is given for the name, surname, rank or profession of the father, nor for the date and place of marriage. The birth certificate has the word 'Illegitimate' printed below the name, Mary Jane Mathieson Kain. We know that Joseph William Wilson was born to Annie Wilson, née McGowan, and Thomas Wilson on 18 June 1879 at Creewood Cottage in Minnigaff. On the evidence of the birth certificates alone, there is no obvious suggestion that the respective families were acquainted, although the places of birth were not all that far apart.

Another source of information is their marriage certificate. As we have already seen, Joseph and Mary Jane married on 2 June 1904 at No. 50 Sciennes, in Edinburgh. At the time, Joseph was living at No. 34 Causewayside and Mary Jane was living at The Farm, Dalzell, Motherwell. Again there is no obvious connection between a Police Constable in Edinburgh and a domestic servant in Motherwell, and yet, some time between their birth and their marriage, Joseph and Mary Jane must have met!

Between the birth dates and the marriage date, we have census forms for 1891 and 1901. At the time of the 1891 census, when Mary Jane would have been 7 years old, she was living at No. 10 Wilton Crescent, Hawick, with her mother, Jane Kain, described as a tweed picker, and her brother, John Kain, aged 3. At the same time, Joseph would have been 11 years of age and living with his family at Balmurrie shepherd's cottage at New Luce. Again there is no obvious connection between the two lifestyles.

However, the 1901 census, as we have seen, places Joseph, aged 22, in digs at No. 105 Causewayside. A further search of the 1901 census unexpectedly revealed details of Mary Jane Kain, aged 17, as a servant at No. 2 Gordon Terrace, Edinburgh, a matter of a mile or so from where Joseph was living. Mary Jane worked as a domestic cook and servant to Alexander M. Milroy, Bank Agent for the British Linen Bank who lived at Gordon Terrace with his wife, Margaret, and children, Jessie (20), Alexander (16), Margaret (15) and Eric (13). Mary Jane may well have attracted the attention of a handsome young Constable, walking the beat in the area where she lived and worked. We will never know: the police records are not sufficiently detailed to say which streets were patrolled by PC Joseph William Wilson. It may well be that Mary Jane's idea of an enforced separation to test Joseph's resolve was implemented by her going away for a year – to Motherwell. It would have been even more intriguing if she had made that announcement just prior to Boxing Day 1902 when Joseph was reprimanded for appearing on duty under the influence of drink.

Alas, my 'meticulous' research was all in vain. Had I only asked that great repository of family information, the fairer sex, I would have discovered at a much earlier stage from my sisters and cousins that Joseph and Mary Jane met at a police ball in Edinburgh. There was even the additional information that Mary Jane actually went to the ball with another policeman as her partner but met Joseph during the course of the evening. Presumably when the beat changed, so did her choice of collar number!

WHO WAS JOSEPH AND MARY JANE'S BRIDESMAID, RACHEL CESSFORD?

The second problem was the identity of Rachel Cessford. As the bridesmaid at a wedding is usually a relative or a friend of the bride, it seemed pointless to try to establish a connection between Rachel and Joseph. She was almost certainly a friend of Mary Jane. To give her her full name, Rachel Liddle Cessford was born at 6.00 am on 2 February 1882 to George Cessford, a ploughman, and his wife, Rachel Cessford, maiden surname Liddle, who were married on 13 August 1869 at South Leith. The birth certificate gives the place of birth as 'Remote Parish of Cranston'. At the time of the 1891 census Rachel Cessford, aged 9, was listed at Remote Farm, Cranston, living with her mother and father, her five sisters and her three brothers. The next reference to Rachel is the 1901 census when she is listed as a 19-year-old servant working for the Simpson family at No. 14 Mayfield Gardens. At the time of the census the head of the household was Mrs George Simpson, her husband having died a few years previously. George Simpson was a wine and spirit merchant with premises at No. 30 Niddry Street in Edinburgh. Rachel and Mary Jane were, therefore, about the same age, in similar employment, and living and working within half a mile of one another. In those days, when servant girls were employed in many of the larger houses in Newington, there were numerous informal groups, often organised by the local churches, which provided support and guidance to domestic staff who were probably away from home and quite vulnerable. It is possible, therefore, that Rachel and Mary Jane met at one of these groups. A further search at New Register House revealed that Rachel Cessford married John P. Moncrieffe of Anstruther on 21 January 1916 and died on 22 April 1962 at the Matthew Fyfe Residential Home in Dunfermline. Unfortunately I was unable to trace descendants of Rachel Liddle Cessford despite advertising in the Dunfermline press.

WHY DO MARY JANE'S PARTICULARS NOT
COINCIDE WITH MY PREVIOUS RESEARCH?

The information on Mary Jane's birth certificate and marriage certificate is difficult to reconcile. Mary Jane was illegitimate and took her mother's surname, Kain, yet on her marriage certificate, her father, said to be deceased at the time of the marriage, is given as Alexander Kain, a grocer, and her mother (also deceased) as Jane Mair (previously Kain) maiden name, Taylor. We now know where the middle name, Mathieson, came from, but it is a mystery why the name Alexander Kain, if he was the father as stated on the marriage certificate, does not also appear on the birth certificate. Alexander Kain, a draper to trade, was, in fact, the name of her mother's brother. Mary Jane claims on her marriage certificate that 'her father', Alexander Kain, was deceased at the time of the marriage, whereas Alexander Kain, her uncle, did not die until 27 April 1911. She also claims on her marriage certificate that her mother's maiden name was Taylor, which is incorrect. Taylor was the maiden name of her maternal grandmother. Mary Jane also omits her middle name, Mathieson, from her marriage certificate. Whilst that may, of itself, be unimportant it is strange that she should have done so in view of the origin of the name in Dumfries where the neighbour, Jane Mathieson, and her family, were helpful to the Kains.

One hundred years after the date of the marriage, it is not possible to know why Mary Jane appears to have given incorrect information on her marriage certificate. She was 20 years of age, embarking on what she hoped would be many years of happy married life, and she obviously wanted to portray herself in the best possible light. There is little doubt that she would have remembered, and been greatly influenced by, her difficult childhood in Dumfries, Hawick and Selkirk. It is even possible that Mary Jane was not aware of all the information which is available to us now. But what she did have, and we do not have, is the experience and recollections of those early traumatic years, especially in Dumfries. Compared to her appalling living conditions in, say, Irish Street in Dumfries, Mary Jane would have thought that her accommodation in Gordon Terrace in Edinburgh was palatial. A servant girl would probably have had a small room (shared with another servant) immediately above the kitchen or in the attic accommodation. Either way, she would have been very comfortable in comparison with her previous situation. It is perfectly possible, and understandable, that Mary Jane decided to give herself something in the nature of a new identity with which to start married life. It is even possible that we now know more about Mary Jane Mathieson Kain than Joseph did when they were about to marry.

WHAT WAS THE SIGNIFICANCE OF NO. 50 SCIENNES?

In the 1902-03 *Edinburgh & Leith Post Office Directory*, four persons are listed at No. 50: William Drysdale; William Forrest; John Walker; and B. C. Hay but there is no evidence to connect any of them with Joseph or Mary Jane. The tenement block, No. 50, still stands at the south end of Sciennes facing along Sciennes Road. The rear windows of the tenement overlook Sciennes Hill House, now incorporated into the tenement flats on the north side of Sciennes House Place. The House is famous for being the location of the only recorded meeting of Robert Burns and Sir Walter Scott in the winter of 1786-87. In 1904, the rear windows of No. 50 also had a good view of the rear of No. 34 Causewayside where Joseph had been in digs.

The Valuation Rolls for 1905-06 list Joseph William Wilson at No. 50 Sciennes which indicates that No. 50 was, in fact, Joseph and Mary Jane's first matrimonial home. A total of eleven houses is listed. The Wilsons' neighbours were from different walks of life, including a fish dealer, blacksmith, compositor, bookbinder and printer. Joseph and Mary Jane paid the smallest rent in the stair, suggesting that theirs was the smallest house, and the Dean of Guild plans for the house when it was built in 1882 show that the smallest houses were on the ground floor. Joseph and Mary Jane were not there for long, however, as the Wilson name does not appear in the 1906-07 Valuation Rolls for No. 50 Sciennes.

At a later stage in my research the significance of the very short stay at No. 50 became evident. The family has always understood that Mary Jane

No. 50 Sciennes in 2004. A century earlier one of the ground-floor flats was the first matrimonial home of Joseph William Wilson and Mary Jane Mathieson Wilson. *Photograph by Phyllis M. Cant.*

may either have given birth to a child while still single (prior to 2 June 1904) or, alternatively, shortly after she was married. It was believed that the child had died in infancy but the place of burial was not known. At New Register House I checked several years under the name 'Kain' without tracing any relevant entries. However, further family enquiry revealed that the child was probably male and that Joseph could have followed the Wilson family tradition and named his first son Thomas. Armed with this information I returned to New Register House and found that looking for a Thomas Wilson in Scotland was slightly more rewarding than looking for a needle in several haystacks. I was encouraged by the official's words: 'If it is there, you will find it.' It was there and I did find it. Thomas Wilson was born at No. 50 Sciennes, Edinburgh at 4.45 pm on Tuesday, 23 May 1905 to Joseph William Wilson, Police Constable, and Mary Jane Wilson, who were married on 2 June 1904. Tracing that entry confirmed that Joseph and Mary Jane's first matrimonial home was No. 50 Sciennes and not No. 2 Braid Place as I had previously thought. Like many other young parents, Joseph and Mary Jane were no doubt delighted with the birth of their first child, who was baptised on Sunday, 9 July 1905. Sadly, during the next month or two young Thomas did not thrive and he died at 8.30 pm on Sunday, 17 December 1905 in his parents' house at No. 50 Sciennes. The death certificate, signed by Charles Kennedy MD, whose practice was at No. 5 Salisbury Road, gave the cause of death as Tabes Mesenterica, a condition which had prevailed for about one month prior to the date of death. Joseph registered the death at Newington Registrar's Office, No. 11 Hope Park Terrace on Monday, 18 December 1905. The entry is signed by the Assistant

This picture, c. 1908, is the earliest photograph discovered of Joseph and Mary Jane together, with their daughter, Jean, who was born on 9 September 1906. *Courtesy of Mrs Grace Thom, née Cant.*

Registrar, William Kirkaldy, with the initials 'J.C.' after the signature. The Registrar was James Craig. Thomas was buried in a private grave in Newington Cemetery at 3.00 pm on Tuesday, 19 December 1905. The records for Newington Cemetery give brief details of the type of funeral conveyance used for each burial, for example, a four-horse hearse. The entry for wee Thomas is much more modest with the single word 'bier', indicating that the small coffin would have been conveyed to the grave on a small timber platform or stand. The bier would be the property of the cemetery company and would only be used within the precincts of Newington Cemetery. No information is available on how the coffin was conveyed from the family home at No. 50 Sciennes to the cemetery gates. The undertaker was William Baillie of No. 231 Causewayside but there are no known details of who attended or the name of the minister who conducted the service. It is very likely to have been the Rev. David A. Rollo of Buccleuch Parish Church. Only parents who have been through this experience can have any idea how Joseph and Mary Jane felt at the loss of their first child. It may well have been the main factor in their deciding to move from No. 50 Sciennes to their second matrimonial home at No. 2 Braid Place, where their second child, Jean, was born on 9 September 1906.

Braid Place and Summerhall Square

After leaving No. 50 Sciennes, Joseph and Mary Jane lived at No. 2 Braid Place and later at No. 8 Summerhall Square. The birth certificates of each of the four surviving children confirm that they were all born at No. 2 Braid Place: Jean, 9 September 1906; Annie, 16 August 1909; Joseph McGowan, 10 May 1915; and John Kain, 27 February 1923. At one time it was thought that the family home was on the south side of the street in the stair nearest to Braid Place Police Station. That, however, is No. 4 whereas all the official evidence confirms that they lived at No. 2 which is the stair furthest away from the Police Station. That side of Braid Place (now Sciennes House Place) has not been redeveloped or renumbered since it was built. No. 2 was a stair, No. 4 was a stair, No. 6 was unallocated (the site of the small Jewish Cemetery), Nos. 8 and 10 were police houses, and No. 12 was Braid Place Police Station. The apparent doubt about the position of the family house was resolved when it was recalled that Annie Wilson or Cant (my mother) had the habit of pointing out the correct house to her offspring when walking between Marchmont Crescent, where we lived, and Priestfield Road, to which Joseph and Mary Jane moved in 1932.

The Valuation Rolls provide confirmation of the street number: Joseph William Wilson is listed at No. 2 Braid Place from 1906. There were 21 houses in the stair, occupied by people with a wide range of occupations, but, surprisingly, no other police officers. There is evidence to suggest that between 1906 and 1928, Mary Jane and Joseph occupied a ground floor flat to begin with and then another flat in the same stair on the second floor. In the 1906–07 Valuation Rolls, Joseph is listed third out of 21 houses. However, by 1921 the rolls (rather conveniently for researchers) had introduced an extra column indicating which tenants lived on which floor. Joseph William Wilson is in thirteenth position, on the second floor.

The tenement, No. 2, containing a mixture of two- and three-apartment houses, was built in 1880 by a small consortium led by George McCathie, an ironmonger, at No. 123 High Street and James Lightbody, a stonemason, of No. 8 Moncrieff Terrace. Many similar tenements in Edinburgh were built in this way by a temporary partnership between experienced tradesmen and businessmen looking for a property investment. In the early years, most of the flats were for let only. No. 50 Sciennes (where Joseph and Mary Jane were married) was built around the same time, the ground plans, dated 1882, showing that the area around Braid Place was due for imminent redevelopment. At the east end of Braid Place (nearest to Causewayside) neither the Fire Station and Public Weigh Machine (on the north side) nor the Police Station (on the south side) had been built. In fact, the eastmost section of what is now Sciennes House Place was a narrow thoroughfare, Jew's Close, giving access, between old tenements, to the small Jewish burial ground which is still on the south side of Braid Place. Braid Place Police Station was not built until 1885. It follows, therefore, that when Joseph and Mary Jane set up home in Braid Place in 1906 the area was relatively modern compared to other parts of Causewayside, with the tenements, Fire Station, Police Station and Public Washhouse (in Causewayside) all built in the previous two decades. Perhaps the most convenient aspect for Joseph was that he was living within a hundred yards of his place of work.

The family was probably at No. 2 Braid Place from around 1906 (after the death of Thomas on 17 December 1905) to 1928. During this period of over twenty years, Joseph made good progress in the service, his weekly wage rising from 30/- (£1.50) per week as a Police Constable, in 1905, to 112/6 (£5.62) as a Sergeant in 1925. His responsibilities were also increasing, with Jean born on 9 September 1906 and Annie on 16 August 1909. Jean was baptised on 16 November 1906 and Annie was baptised by the Rev. James E. Houston of Buccleuch Parish Church on Tuesday, 30 November 1909. Less than two years later, on Sunday, 16 July 1911, Mary Jane decided to join the Baptist Church in Duncan Street, off Causewayside. Baptism in the Baptist Church was, and still is, by complete immersion in the water in the tank, or pool, at the front of the church. Mary Jane would probably have been dressed in a swimming costume and covered by a white shroud or cloak. The minister, the Rev. George Douglas, assisted by one deacon, would also have been in the water in the church's baptismal tank to conduct

Mary Jane Mathieson Wilson in pensive mood at an unidentified location, probably around the time of the First World War. *Courtesy of Mrs Grace Thom, née Cant.*

OPPOSITE. Joseph and Mary Jane at an unknown location probably in the 1920s. Although the original photograph is badly damaged, it seems to have been taken on the day of a fairly formal occasion, perhaps a wedding. Mary Jane's hat appears to be lying on the ground to the left of the bench. *Courtesy of Mrs Grace Thom, née Cant.*

ABOVE LEFT. Joseph and Mary Jane, *c.* 1925, with their son, John, who was born on 27 February 1923. *Courtesy of Mrs Grace Thom, née Cant.*

ABOVE RIGHT. Mary Jane Mathieson Wilson, on the left, with her daughter Annie, probably in the Meadows, Edinburgh, *c.* 1925. The child playing on the grass is John Kain Wilson, born 27 February 1923. *Courtesy of Mrs Grace Thom, née Cant.*

the ceremony. Mary Jane appears to have allowed her attendance to decline during 1916, and she ceased to be a member on 15 June 1916. We do not know why this came about, slightly more than one year after Joseph, junior, was born on 15 June 1915, and (as far as we can ascertain) four months before her brother, John, died at the Somme on 12 October 1916.

The house at No. 2 was not without its own share of tragedy: Joseph and Mary Jane had another child who died in infancy. Mary Wilson was born at No. 2 Braid Place at 6.15 pm on Tuesday, 16 March 1920, and tragically died the same night at 10.55 pm. There is no record of Mary ever having been baptised. The death certificate, signed by J. L. Green MD, of No. 23 Minto Street, gives the cause of death as 'Post Natal Haemoptysis' and the duration of the disease as four and a half hours. Joseph registered the birth and the death at Newington Registrar's Office at No. 16 East Preston Street on the following day Wednesday, 17 March 1920. Mary was buried beside her older brother, Thomas, in Newington Cemetery at 2.30 pm on Thursday, 18 March 1920. Again, William Baillie was the undertaker but there is no information available as to who was present at the interment, nor the name of the minister who conducted the service. When Mary died, her older sister Jean was 13 years of age, Annie was 10 and Joseph was 4. The youngest member of the family, John Kain, was born at No. 2 Braid Place on 27 February 1923.

The Wilson family remained at No. 2 Braid Place until around 1928 when they moved to No. 8 Summerhall Square. The property was owned by Robert Sharp and had eight houses in the stair, the average annual rental being £23. At that time, Joseph was earning just over £300 per annum as a Police Sergeant. Unfortunately, I was not able to locate the building plans for the tenement (built prior to 1876) which would have given more detailed information on the layout of the house.

Joseph and Mary Jane's older daughter, Jean, was 22 when she married George McIntosh Johnstone, aged 24, at the family home in Summerhall Square on 1 June 1929. The wedding ceremony was taken by the Rev. William Morgan Robertson Rusk, minister of Hope Park United Free Church. The bridesmaid was Jean's younger sister, Annie Wilson, and the best man was Edward Campbell Robertson, who was engaged to Annie at the time.

The Wilsons remained at Summerhall Square until 1932 when Joseph bought his first house at Priestfield Road. At one time my research indicated that Joseph William Wilson and his family may have returned for a short while to No. 2 Braid Place before going to Priestfield Road, but this has proved to be inaccurate. By an unfortunate coincidence from a researcher's point of view, shortly before Joseph William Wilson moved away from No. 2 Braid Place in 1928, a gentleman by the name of James Watt Wilson moved into No. 2 and was listed in the *Edinburgh and Leith Post Office Directories* as 'J. W. Wilson': hence the confusion.

Joseph and Mary Jane's oldest child, Jean, married George McIntosh Johnstone at the family home in Summerhall Square on 1 June 1929. The bridesmaid was the bride's younger sister, Annie, and the best man was Edward Campbell Robertson. *Courtesy of Mrs Jean Stewart, née Wilson.*

In Search of a Man without Boots

The police records, already referred to, provide further details of Joseph's progress while he was living at Braid Place and Summerhall Square. On 3 January 1905, a matter of six months after he was married, Joseph received a further advancement 'from 1st grade 2nd class to 4th grade 1st class', and on 11 December 1906 he received an Award for Meritorious Conduct:

> P.C. 401 Joseph Wilson – Awarded ten shillings for tact and discretion shewn in apprehending a suspect who turned out to be a K.T. and was convicted under the Prevention of Crimes Act.

Joseph's undoubted 'tact and discretion' had obviously been used to great advantage in the arrest of an important member of society, the letters 'KT' usually denoting the title of Knight of the Most Ancient and Most Noble Order of the Thistle. Imagine my chagrin on learning that in police terminology the letters 'KT' stand for 'Known Thief'. Meritorious conduct none the less, and the ten shillings would have been a welcome addition to the household budget, coming just three months after the birth of Joseph and Mary Jane's second child, Jean, on 9 September 1906. The Award for Meritorious Conduct was quickly followed by another advancement on 1 January 1907 'from 4th to 3rd grade 1st class'. I was not able to trace the advancement from 3rd to 2nd grade but on 4 January 1910 Joseph received '1st grade 1st class'. By that time his second daughter, Annie, had been born, on 16 August 1909. Joseph was born on 10 May 1915 and John on 27 February 1923.

On 18 May 1920 Joseph was promoted to the rank of Sergeant and was transferred to West End Police Station, initially as PS 66. Progress through the various grades came annually: 1921, 5th; 1922, 4th; 1923, 3rd; 1924, 2nd; and finally 1925, 1st. Sometime around 1922 Joseph's collar number was

OPPOSITE. PC 401 of C Division, Joseph William Wilson, at the south-east end of Dick Place in the Grange district of Edinburgh. According to *History of the Lothians & Borders Police* the arm badge is 'a class or grade one P. C. arm badge' in use between 1890 and 1935. Joseph received his promotion to Grade 4 Class 1 on 3 January 1905 and reached Grade 1 on 4 January 1910. If it was a celebratory photograph then it was probably taken in 1905. *Courtesy of Andrew Wilson.*

changed from PS 66 to PS 96 but again no explanation could be found for this. However, from the early 1920s the style of the Weekly Reports was considerably altered to include lengthy accounts of the circumstances in which individual officers were considered for Commendations. One such report is from Superintendent Colin Brown of D Division, West End Station to the Chief Constable's Office:

> For the favourable consideration of the Chief Constable, Inspr. Jas. Mackay begs to report on the alertness and attention to duty displayed by P. S. 96 Joseph Wilson, in the arrest of Alexander Mackay, (23) labourer, 1 St David's Terrace, on a charge of having been seen on premises with intent to commit theft, the particulars of which are as follows:

> At 12-25 am Saturday 21st May, 1927, information was circulated from C.I. Department to the effect that a man had been seen inside the grounds of a temporary unoccupied dwelling-house at 41 Polwarth Terrace, and as he had left his boots beside said house, he was suspected of having been there with the intention of committing a crime.
>   Sergeant Wilson, who was in his Station, when the information came through, went out in search of a man without boots, and at 12-35 am same date, on observing accused in Grove Street, only about 200 yards from his house, arrested him, and brought him to this Station, where he was charged accordingly.
>   Accused, who had been before the Court on a former occasion, for a similar offence, was on Wednesday 25th instant, at the City Police Court, sentenced for the offence to 30 days' imprisonment.
>   There is no doubt but for the alertness of Sergt. Wilson in arresting this man, there would be considerable difficulty in tracing and convicting this man if he had been able to reach his home, and provide himself with another pair of boots.

It is respectfully requested that this report be submitted for the information of the Chief Constable.

The report was submitted on 26 May 1927 by James Mackay, Inspector, to the Superintendent, Colin Brown, who in turn submitted it to the Chief Constable. The report bears the circular stamp of the Chief Constable's Office and has the word 'Commended' written by the Chief Constable and initialled. Having read several similar accounts in the Weekly Reports concerning other officers, it never ceases to amaze me how many would-be villains were arrested after their boots were seen left outside the scene of the crime.

By the following year, 1928, Joseph was within two years of retirement but it is clear that he was by no means desk-bound. A further lengthy report and Commendation appears on 23 April 1928:

> For the favourable consideration of the Chief Constable, Inspr. Jas. Mackay begs to report on the alertness and attention to duty displayed by P. S. 96 Joseph Wilson and P. C. 534 James Liney, in the arrest of John McLellan Miller, (23) baker, 55 Springbank Street, Maryhill, Glasgow, c/o Weir, and James McGavin (19) labourer, 18 Calton Hill, Edinburgh, c/o Mulholland, on a charge of having been found in the doorway of premises with intent to commit theft, the particulars of which are as follows:
>
> At 12.50 am Wednesday 18th April 1927 Sergeant Wilson and Constable Liney, who were on duty in Dalry Road, observed the accused acting in a suspicious manner in said street. They kept the men under observation and saw them conceal themselves in the doorway of the shop at 43 Dalry Road, occupied by Antonia Tartaglia, Restaurateur there. The doorway at the time was very dark, and the fanlight window above the door partly open for the purpose of ventilation.
>
> On going forward to the doorway the Officers found Miller on the top of a wooden ash-bucket about two feet high, and McGavin keeping watch on the street.

The Sergeant and Constable took the men into custody, and when accused were charged in the West End Police Station with being found in said doorway with intent to commit theft, the accused McGavin admitted being there for the purpose, while the accused Miller denied the charge.

Both accused when brought before the City Police Court plead guilty to the charge and on Saturday 21st April 1928, the accused Miller, who had been previously convicted for theft by Housebreaking in Aberdeen, was sentenced for this offence to 60 days' imprisonment, and the accused McGavin, who had been previously convicted for dishonest appropriation of property at Dundee was sentenced for the offence to 30 days' imprisonment.

There is no doubt but for the alertness of Sergeant Wilson and Constable Liney in observing the suspicious actions of these men, they would have entered the premises referred to by way of the fanlight window, this being the manner in which Miller entered the premises at Aberdeen, and there would have been considerable difficulty in tracing them if they had got clear of the premises.

It is respectfully requested that the report be submitted for the information of the Chief Constable.

The report bears the stamp of the Chief Constable's Office, the date 8/5/28 and the word 'Commended'.

Towards the end of Joseph's career in the Edinburgh City Police, he took on the duties of Acting Inspector at the West End Station. I understand that an 'acting' rank is not a formal promotion and no date is shown in the Weekly Reports. However, reference is made to Acting Inspector Joseph Wilson in a Commendation report submitted on 24 August 1930 for PC 530 Walter Hughes. The report is signed 'J W. Wilson, A/Inspector' and is the only example of Joseph's handwriting which I was able to trace.

After studying the Police Weekly Records, I located a volume which was described simply as 'Surnames W' which turned out to be very much more informative than the description suggested. As well as confirming the information already gleaned, it recorded physical characteristics: Height, 6ft.1; Chest, – ; Hair, Fair; Eyes, Blue; Complexion, Fair; Marks, –. It also gave details of Joseph's weekly wage between 1900 and 1925. Earning capacity is always a comparative study but it is interesting to consider that Joseph was earning: 30/- (£1.50) per week when Jean was born on 9 September 1906; 32/- (£1.60) per week when Annie was born on 16 August 1909; 37/4 (£1.87) when Joe was born on 10 May 1915; and 100/- (£5) when John was born on 27 February 1923. Even when Joseph retired in 1930 his wage was almost certainly less than £7 per week.

The same volume (Surnames W) gives details of Joseph's sickness record between 1902 and 1928 in which there are a variety of ailments, some of which were probably associated with the all-weather nature of the job. The list is probably most significant for what it does not reveal. Many of my generation in the family recall that Joseph suffered for many years from an injury to his shin, allegedly caused by a drunk, who, in the course of being arrested, had kicked out at Joseph. If that had been the cause, its absence from the list of ailments is surprising. If the injury had been caused in a domestic situation it would not need to be disclosed to Joseph's employer.

The final entry in the Police Weekly Records relating to Joseph is short and to the point, marking the end of a very satisfactory police career of over 30 years.

23.9.30
Retiral on Pension. P.S. 96 Joseph W. Wilson on 22nd inst.

When Joseph retired he was 51 years of age and was living at No. 8 Summerhall Square with his wife Mary Jane. Their eldest daughter, Jean, was already married (1 June 1929) but Annie, aged 21, Joseph McGowan, aged 15, and John Kain, aged 7, were still at home.

The Call of Home

While Joseph was making progress with his career in the police and bringing up his family in the Causewayside area of Edinburgh, he did not forget about his strong family ties in the south-west of Scotland. The last family home, where all nine children were reared, was Balmurrie shepherd's cottage which the Wilson family left around 1897 to go to Cairnholy in Kirkcudbrightshire.

The farm house at Cairnholy formed one side of a courtyard which lay in a sheltered, natural hollow in the ground a few hundred yards beyond the standing stones. The earliest record that I could trace of the Wilsons at Cairnholy was the Valuation Rolls for 1897-98. The owner is given as Christian Robison McCulloch Jameson, wife of Andrew Jameson, an advocate in Edinburgh. The tenants and occupiers are listed as: Thomas Wilson, senior; Thomas Wilson, junior; and John (Jeck) McGowan Wilson; farmers. The reference to Thomas Wilson junior suggests that when Thomas senior and the family moved from Balmurrie, Thomas junior must have left Shennanton, Kirkcowan where he had been working at the time of the 1891 census. By 1901, the census return for the Wilsons at Cairnholy (spelt Cairnholly), described as one house with eight rooms with one or more windows, is as follows:

Thomas Wilson		Head	Married	65	Farmer	Employer	born Ayrshire, Barr
Annie	Do.	Wife	Married	55	Farmer's wife	–	born Minnigaff
John McG.	Do.	Son	S	27	Cattleman	Worker	born Minnigaff
Margt. M.	Do.	Daur.	S	23	Poultry Keeper	Worker	born Minnigaff
Robert	Do.	Son	S	19	Ploughman	Worker	born Minnigaff
Annie	Do.	Daur.	S	17	Farm Domestic	Worker	born Colmonell
William	Do.	Son	S	15	Shepherd	Worker	born New Luce
Agnes	Do.	Daur	S	12	Scholar	–	born New Luce

Of the nine known siblings, only six are recorded. One of these, Joseph, we already know was at No. 105 Causewayside in Edinburgh, but, surprisingly, Thomas junior and James are not recorded at Cairnholy in 1901. Thomas junior was at Markdow Farm, New Luce, working for Margaret Dodd, a farmer's widow, and James had probably already left Cairnholy to join the Bootle police.

No letters or post cards between Joseph and his family have survived for us to gauge the extent of contact between them, but we do know that Robert travelled to Edinburgh to be the best man at the wedding of Joseph and Mary Jane on 2 June 1904. Just over four years later, on 24 July 1908, Joseph's father died at Cairnholy, the cause of death on the certificate being 'Supposed Syncope'. His death certificate and his tombstone in the churchyard of Kirkmabreck Parish Church both give his age as 73, but according to the Old Parochial Register for the Parish of Barr, Ayrshire, he was born on 19 May 1832 and baptised on 22 June. If both official records are correct, then he was 76 when he died. The doubt about his age at date of death does not, however, detract from the intrinsically interesting photograph of him sitting quietly in the garden at Cairnholy with his widow and nine children on the day of his funeral! Thanks to the wonders of modern photography in 1908, the Newton Stewart photographers, W. Hunter & Son, came to Cairnholy to take a series of photographs and later 'set in' a previous photograph of Thomas so as to look as though he was

The complete Wilson family, father, mother, six sons and three daughters all appear in this photograph in July 1908 at Cairnholy, Kirkcudbrightshire – despite the fact that the father, Thomas Wilson, had died a few days previously. Thanks to the ingenuity of the photographers, W. Hunter & Son of Newton Stewart, a previous picture of Thomas Wilson was set into the picture of the family group taken on the day of the funeral. From left to right, back row: Thomas Jnr, Jeck, Bob, Jim, Joseph and William. Front row: Peggie, Thomas (inset), Annie (mother), Annie and Agnes. *Courtesy of John Wilson of Kirkmabreck.*

Three generations of the Hunter family, members of St Ninian's Lodge, No. 499, left to right: Charles Hunter; Past Master, William Hunter; and William Hunter. The Hunter family, who took the Cairnholy photographs, were photographers in Newton Stewart from at least 1878. *Courtesy of The Museum, Newton Stewart.*

OPPOSITE. The six Wilson brothers were also photographed in the garden at Cairnholy on the day of their father's funeral in July 1908. Left to right, back row: Thomas, Jeck and Jim. Front row: Joseph, Bob and William. *Courtesy of John Wilson of Kirkmabreck.*

sitting in the family group beside his widow, Annie. Only the position of his feet reveal the truth: in the photograph they are not quite on the ground but, in reality, they were already *in* the ground – at Kirkmabreck churchyard! I understand that the practice of adding in the deceased to a group photograph was unusual in 1908 but not unknown. William Hunter junior was working as a photographer at No. 18 Victoria Terrace, Newton Stewart, from 1878, and the firm became William Hunter & Son in 1907.

At the time of Thomas' death, Joseph was living at No. 2 Braid Place with his wife, Mary Jane, and their daughter Jean aged nearly 2 years. Not long after the death of Thomas senior, Thomas junior, and his younger brother, Robert, emigrated to New Zealand in 1910. This must have been a great sadness for their mother, Annie, who by this time was 64 and had already lost her husband and the direct support of Joseph, who had joined the Edinburgh police, and James who had joined the Bootle police. She

OPPOSITE. The three daughters were also photographed in the garden at Cairnholy on the day of their father's funeral in July 1908. Left to right: Peggie, Annie and Agnes.
Courtesy of John Wilson of Kirkmabreck.

ABOVE. A Wilson family photograph taken at Kirkdale School, Carsluith, *c.* 1928. From left to right: Nancy, Annie, Tam and Jean. When the photograph was taken the Wilsons lived at Blackmyre and walked to and from the school each day, a distance of over two miles.
Courtesy of Mrs Jean Stewart née Wilson.

did, however, have very able assistance from her remaining sons, John (Jeck) and William, and her three daughters, Margaret (Peggie), Annie and Agnes. Annie senior died aged 70 at Cairnholy on 6 July 1916 and was buried beside her husband in Kirkmabreck churchyard. Her death certificate gives the cause of death as 'Malignant disease of Breast' and the duration of her illness as one year and six months. When Annie died, Joseph and Mary Jane were at No. 2 Braid Place, in Edinburgh, with their three children: Jean was nearly 10; Annie was nearly 7; and Joseph junior, was just over 1 year old. It is known that Joseph and Mary Jane and their family made frequent visits to Cairnholy around this time as both Jean and Annie were in the habit of recalling to their own families the enjoyable journeys to visit 'Grannie McGowan'. Apparently they took the train to Creetown railway station and horse and trap from there, along what is now the approximate line of the A75 road, to Cairnholy farm house. In 1919, the remaining siblings moved to Kirkmabreck Farm and Blackmyre. John, or Jeck (who was still unmarried) and his sisters, Margaret (Peggie), Annie and Agnes went to Kirkmabreck farm house, and William, who had married

Jane Jamieson in 1917, set up house with their two eldest children, Jean and Tam, at the shepherd's cottage at Blackmyre, two miles from Kirkmabreck.

Around 1926, at the time of the General Strike, James was still in the Bootle police when the rank and file were given strict orders not to follow the strike but to return to work within a given deadline. The story goes that James' communist beliefs prevented him from obeying the command and he was either sacked or left under a cloud. He decided to take his wife and family to New Zealand to join his brothers, Thomas and Robert, where he remained until his death in 1966 at the age of 91. It is very likely that James and Joseph would have met up before the emigration date but sadly we have no record of that. We do know, however, from the clear recollection of Jean Stewart (née Wilson) of Creetown that James, accompanied by one of his daughters, came to Blackmyre (and presumably Kirkmabreck) to say his farewells to his brothers and sisters. At the time Jean was only 6 years of age but remembers the occasion well.

James (Jim), one of Joseph's older brothers, was born at Creewood Cottage on 10 October 1875. After service in the Bootle police, he emigrated to New Zealand, *c.* 1926, where he died on 17 October 1966, aged 91. *Courtesy of John Wilson of Kirkmabreck.*

PRIESTFIELD, EDINBURGH
AND THOUGHTS OF HOME

My earliest recollection of my grandfather's home was at No. 57 Priestfield Road. I think that most of the present family agree that the house was the 'spiritual' home of the Edinburgh branch of the Wilson family. My grandfather bought the house in 1932 when it was newly built, but he would probably have known the district from about 1900 when he joined the Edinburgh City Police as a young Constable attached to Braid Place Police Station.

Priestfield Road was constructed on part of the estate of Prestonfield House which was built in the seventeenth century for Sir James Dick, Lord Provost of Edinburgh. Like many similar grand houses near Edinburgh, its history is characterised by a gradual reduction in the size of the surrounding estate as various parts were sold off for housing. Kirkwood's Map of 1817 shows Dalkeith Road (unnamed) following about the same alignment as it does today. The small hamlet of Rosehall is shown about the position of present-day Priestfield Church (previously Rosehall Church), and Echo Bank is shown further down Dalkeith Road, on the east side, near present-day Prestonfield Avenue. Also on the east side of Dalkeith Road, at a point about mid-way between Rosehall and Echo Bank, two small lodges are shown, described as Prestonfield Gate, giving access to a long curving driveway to Prestonfield House. The position of the driveway is substantially similar to the alignment of Priestfield Road today. Shortly before 1876 important changes occurred in the layout of the part of the Prestonfield House estate nearest to Dalkeith Road. The lodges at Prestonfield Gate

A muzzled, performing bear with its keeper in Priestfield Road North with Salisbury Crags in the background, 1895. *From the Malcolm Cant Collection.*

were removed about the same time as the construction of the tenement building which included No. 139 Dalkeith Road. This tenement, immediately to the north of the junction with Priestfield Road, was erected in 1877, but unfortunately the plans, which might have included a ground plan of the area, have not survived. In 1876 a new lodge house, which still exists, was erected on the corner of Priestfield Road North and Priestfield Road. Beyond the lodge house, the estate of Prestonfield House lay in complete seclusion, that is, until the early 1930s when the owner of the estate, Sir William Stewart Dick-Cunnynghame, Baronet, granted a feu of land to Thomas L. Rae & Company to build bungalows on an extended section of Priestfield Road.

On 24 June 1932 Thomas L. Rae & Company, builders, of No. 17 York Place, Edinburgh were given permission by the Dean of Guild Court to erect a further phase of fourteen bungalows in Priestfield Road and Priestfield Grove: two Type A houses; six Type B houses; and six Type C houses. The ground plan for the position of the houses on the north-east side of Priestfield Road (nearest to Arthur's Seat) has the names of the prospective buyers written informally against each plot: No. 49 Type B, Cockburn; No. 51 Type C, Ferguson; No. 53 Type B, McLean; and No. 55 Type C, Suttie. No. 57, which was bought by my grandfather, was Type B, and certified as finished on 24 December 1932, but his name does not appear on the ground plan. The omission is not significant as names were not always inserted and there were frequent changes when prospective buyers changed their minds about which house they wanted. No. 57 had an added amenity for some time after it was built as it was the last house to be erected in that phase and therefore had an open outlook on the south side until other houses were completed. When my grandfather bought No. 57 he must have been very proud of his achievement. All his childhood years had been spent in very modest cottages, and when he came to Edinburgh he lived in fairly small accommodation at Causewayside, Sciennes and Braid Place, before securing the tenancy of a bigger house at Summerhall Square. But to have his own detached house, with a magnificent view of Arthur's Seat, must have been a dream come true. He had not long retired from the police force and he was getting to the stage where his family was becoming more independent. With the help of a loan of £490 from the Leeds Permanent Building Society my grandfather bought No. 57 for £663 on 29 December 1932. There was only one thing more to do and that was to give the house a name. He called it Cairnholy after the farm at Cairnholy, Kirkcudbrightshire where his mother and father, and his brothers and sisters lived when he left Galloway to come to Edinburgh in 1900. Although the name was obviously important to him I have often wondered why he chose Cairnholy and not Minnigaff, Creewood, Lochton or Balmurrie. Perhaps he just liked the sound of the name best. He had actually lived at Creewood, Lochton and Balmurrie but he did not go to Cairnholy with the rest of the family after they left Balmurrie, New Luce. He stayed behind at a neighbouring farm Balneil, New Luce, and went to Edinburgh from there. No doubt he visited Cairnholy to say farewell to his

From the papers of the late George S. Cant

family and must have had very mixed feelings as to whether or not he was doing the right thing. He could never have imagined that, many decades later, a memento which he probably brought from Cairnholy Farm to Edinburgh would again surface in the most unexpected manner.

No. 57 Priestfield Road was the home from which three of his four surviving children were married. The elder daughter, Jean, had married George McIntosh Johnstone on 1 June 1929 when the family was still at No. 8 Summerhall Square and the second daughter, Annie, married William Stoddart Cant on 11 February 1936 at Fountainbridge Church. Joseph McGowan, the elder son, married Georgina Torrance Turnbull on 22 June 1946 at Holyrood Abbey Church, and John Kain, the younger son, married Marion Cochrane Mather Stewart on 27 February 1954 at St Cuthbert's Parish Church at the West End of Edinburgh.

OPPOSITE. Annie Wilson (the author's mother) photographed by Drummond Shiels, photographers, of Nos 70 and 72 Lauriston Place, Edinburgh, in December 1933.

ABOVE. On the steps of Holyrood Abbey Church, Edinburgh, on 22 June 1946, at the marriage of Georgina Torrance Turnbull and Joseph McGowan Wilson. The best man was John Kain Wilson, the groom's brother, and the bridesmaid was Janet McKinnon Balsillie. *Courtesy of Andrew Wilson.*

A large group of family and friends at the wedding of Georgina and Joseph (Georgie and Joe) on 22 June 1946. *Courtesy of Andrew Wilson.*

1	Joseph William Wilson	7	Joseph McGowan Wilson	14	Not identified
2	Janie Turnbull	8	Andrew Turnbull	15	Grace Cant
3	Edith Taylor	9	Emily Turnbull	16	Dorothy Johnstone
4	Mary Jane Mathieson Wilson	10	Janet Balsillie	17	Mary Cant
		11	Annie Cant	18	Malcolm Cant
5	John Kain Wilson	12	Mary Johnstone	19	Sheila Johnstone
6	Georgina Wilson	13	Not identified	20	Not identified

My earliest recollection of my grandfather's house would be about 1945 when I was five years of age. I remember that as a child I thought my grandfather was a very quiet, thoughtful and somewhat distant character who always seemed to be in his gardening clothes and smoking a pipe. My grandmother was quite different. She was always bustling about and giving instructions but as she also controlled the endless supply of jammed pancakes, German biscuits, ice cream and bottles of lemonade, I thought that I should do nothing that would upset her. As I grew older, and certainly by the time I was in my early teens, it began to dawn on me that she was not quite as kindly as I had first thought, particularly to my grandfather and other adults around her. I think I was really quite slow to notice this, considerably slower than my sisters and female cousins. That seems to be the way young boys are. Perhaps I was influenced by the pancakes.

From about 1939 to 1956 the Cant family lived in the top flat of No. 39 Marchmont Crescent from where we were in the habit of walking to Priestfield Road on a fairly regular basis. I remember the route as though it were yesterday: down Marchmont Crescent to Loch, the grocer, and along Roseneath Street into Sciennes Road where we passed the Sick Children's Hospital and Sciennes Primary School, both of which were important to me. I have a very hazy recollection of being in the Sick Children's Hospital for an operation prior to school age, and being carried home to No. 39 Marchmont Crescent by my father. On reflection, that must be the closest we ever got. I have a much clearer memory of attending Sciennes Primary School for the first time. Many of the mothers were present, no doubt the younger ones anxious about leaving their offspring and the older ones more than relieved to do so. Some of the girls were crying and most of the boys. The only difference I can recall between me and the other boys is that they cried when their mothers left them and I cried when mine came back to collect me. Alas, I know not why, but I have no doubt that on our way to Priestfield Road we would tell and retell many similar anecdotes. The route took us past Tommy Teviotdale's small general store in Sciennes and round the corner into Braid Place where my mother, if she was with us, was in the habit of pointing out the ground-floor flat at No. 2 Braid Place where she was born. At the end of Braid Place we passed the Police Station (where my grandfather had been a Constable), crossed Causewayside, and went up a

A family group in the garden of No. 57 Priestfield Road, Edinburgh, *c.* 1945. Standing, left to right: Annie Cant, Malcolm Cant and Granny Wilson. Sitting, left to right: Grace Cant, Georgina Wilson and Mary Cant. *Courtesy of Mrs Mary Sneddon, née Cant.*

wee lane with the public washhouse on the left and a cabinetmaker's business premises on the right. I remember being intrigued by the waft of hot steamy air coming out of the washhouse but I was not tall enough to see in through the high grilled windows. We crossed Newington Road, walked up Salisbury Road past the synagogue, and down Dalkeith Road. At Rosehall Church, which my grandfather and grandmother attended, we went by way of Marchhall Road where the houses were much grander and, to us, quite intimidating even though we were only walking past on the pavement. When I was quite young there was one house which particularly fascinated me, and that was the lodge house on the corner of Priestfield Road North and Priestfield Road. It had a date, 1876, on the side of it and a brass name plate with the owner's name, Johnston, in block capitals. Mr Johnston was the greenkeeper at Prestonfield Golf Course. The name on the brass plate always reminded me of my cousins, the Johnstones, who lived at No. 55 next door to my grandfather. On arrival at No. 57 the comparatively long walk was rewarded by a selection of Granny Wilson's

Grandpa Wilson, every inch a
man of the soil, complete with
dibber and seedlings. Hopefully,
no lingering pipe smoke got back
in through the open window!
Courtesy of Andrew Wilson.

home baking – sometimes still hot from the oven or the girdle.

My grandfather was usually in the garden, smoking his pipe, and often
looking wistfully at Salisbury Crags and the great haunch of Arthur's Seat.
I thought that that was just how grandpas were. At the bottom of the
garden on the other side of the boundary railings, there was a rough piece
of ground adjacent to Prestonfield Golf Course and the policies of Prestonfield House, which was still a private house. The owners kept peacocks in
the grounds which often came right up to the boundary railings. On
grandpa's side of the railings he grew blackcurrants, gooseberries,
strawberries and rows and rows of runner beans and garden peas. We called
them peapods. Granny would come out and regardless of whether the crop
was ready or not would demand that Grandpa produce some 'berries for
the bairns'. Even at that age I remember thinking that it was hardly his fault
if the sun hadn't shone that week but Granny did not seem to take that into
account. Before the end of our visit we were usually sent down to Mr
Arthur, the grocer, for whatever Granny had run out of. Most things were

Grandpa Wilson, Georgina Wilson and her cousin, Irene, in the garden at No. 57 Priestfield Road, *c.* 1948. The grandchildren on the right, in order of height, are Andrew Wilson, George Johnstone, Dorothy Johnstone and Sheila Johnstone. *Courtesy of Mrs Sheila Henderson, née Johnstone.*

rather boring, such as lentils, oatmeal and self-raising flour, but others, like bottles of lemonade, seemed to be more important to us. What I liked most about the shop was that Mr Arthur never seemed to want any money for what we bought. As we left the shop, fully laden, all he ever said was: 'Are you sure you're Mrs Wilson's grandchildren?' I never thought that there could have been any doubt about that. I now know, of course, that everything would have had to be paid for when the account came in at the end of the week.

I am fairly sure that many of my cousins will have similar memories of No. 57 but it has to be said that the more senior members of the family have very clear memories of less happy times when my grandmother engaged in her frequent tantrums, usually directed at my grandfather. Everyone concerned will have their own experiences and our judgments must be individual and subjective, but there is no doubt about the unhappiness which resulted from these outbursts which were often accompanied by physical assaults on whomever was in the line of fire.

My grandfather was at No. 57 Priestfield Road for one day less than 24

LEFT. Granny and Grandpa Wilson in the garden at No. 57 Priestfield Road, 1957.
Courtesy of Andrew Wilson.

BELOW. From left to right: Grandpa Wilson, Granny Wilson holding her granddaughter, Kathleen, and Georgina Wilson, with Andrew looking on from the doorway. The photograph was taken on holiday at Biggar in June 1949.
Courtesy of Andrew Wilson.

years, which should have been one of the most enjoyable periods of his life. He had completed 30 satisfactory years in the police force where he had reached the position of Acting Inspector at West End Police Station. He had bought a very comfortable house with a view which may well have reminded him of his early years in Galloway. He had taken a small job as doorman at the Caledonian Hotel at the West End, he had joined Lutton

OPPOSITE. John Kain Wilson and Marion Wilson on their wedding day, 27 February 1954, at St Cuthbert's Parish Church at the West End of Edinburgh. The traditional horseshoe is being presented by Myra Brown. *Courtesy of Mrs Marion Wilson, née Stewart.*

ABOVE. Marion Wilson with her sons, Stewart on the left and Alister on the right, at West Savile Terrace in 1959. *Courtesy of Mrs Marion Wilson, née Stewart.*

Place Bowling Club, and he was an ardent supporter of the Hearts, at Tynecastle. He enjoyed his garden and smoking Erinmore Flake tobacco, a habit which did not endear him to everyone, especially when it was accompanied by spitting in the coal fire. My grandmother, rightly, took exception to this, particularly when his aim was not as accurate as it should have been. By 1954, his children had all married and in due course there were 14 grandchildren, 13 of whom were born in his lifetime. No close relative had died during the Second World War, and post-war there were frequent family gatherings, for example, in 1953 when all the cousins sat in the living-room to watch the Coronation of Queen Elizabeth II on television. In those days television sets were much more rudimentary than they are now. The picture was in black and white and could only be seen properly in daylight if the curtains were closed to restrict the amount of light. In addition to that, the enjoyment of the programme was frequently

Not quite the World Cup, only a preliminary stage: Roderick Cant, on the right, and Malcolm Cant at No. 31 Redford Loan in the early 1960s.

spoiled by the intermittent and unannounced 'rolling' of the picture, which, with dexterity, could be controlled by a small knob at the back of the set called 'vertical hold'. For some obscure reason, the manufacturers of television sets in the early days placed the vertical hold control in such a position that it was almost impossible to use it and see the screen at the same time.

The following year, 1954, was an important time for the family: on 27 February John and Marion were married on John's 31st birthday; on 2 June Granny and Grandpa Wilson celebrated their golden wedding anniversary, and on 18 June my grandfather celebrated his 75th birthday. In retrospect I believe my grandfather's reflective, wistful demeanour in general may well have had deeper roots than were evident at the time. For certain he never forgot his close associations with Galloway and he may well have wondered whether he had made the right decision in coming to Edinburgh. In his later years he would also have reflected on what might have been if two of his children, Thomas and Mary, had lived past infancy. They both lay in the same grave in Newington Cemetery only half a mile from his house. To my knowledge he never spoke about them to any member of the present family, nor even pointed out where they were buried.

In 1956 my grandfather was 77 years of age but still in reasonable health, and as far as I am aware not in any financial difficulties. Apparently he considered, but rejected, his family's suggestion to buy a small flat in Blackwood Crescent and to sell No. 57. At the end of that year he advertised No. 57 Priestfield Road for sale and it was bought by the Jones family on 28 December for £2,300. The story might well have ended there but for an uncanny quirk in my research. In April 2004 I was in the process of putting together all the information which I had gathered on No. 57 and I was again looking through the legal papers which had been traced. In 1956, No. 57 was bought by Jane Jones, Edward Jones and Anne Pringle Jones, and as recently as 1994 there had been a further transfer of interest within the Jones family. It was just possible that I would be able to trace the Jones family if my prowess as a researcher was up to the challenge. Fortunately it was not put to any great test. Edward Jones was still listed in the Edinburgh and Lothians telephone book at No. 57 Priestfield Road. I thought that I had better phone him. When I explained the nature of my enquiry, Mr Jones said that if I wanted to see the house I would need to move quickly as he was moving out shortly. After a lapse of nearly 50 years I arranged, with some trepidation, to visit my grandfather's house at 7.15 pm on Wednesday, 21 April 2004. It was a very strange experience. Despite having already been inundated by surveyors and prospective buyers, Mr and Mrs Jones kindly showed me round the house and garden. The rooms were used in substantially the same way as in my grandfather's time, with a sitting-room and bedroom at the front, another bedroom to the side of the house, and the main living-room and kitchen to the rear. The lobby press, with the high door handle, was opposite the living-room door. Granny's kitchen presses, or cupboards, now modernised, were in the same position, the one nearest to the outer wall of the house still being fitted with the 'larder', originally used for the milk. This was a very innovative feature of 1930s bungalows in Edinburgh. It was about one foot square, built into the thickness of the outer wall, and protected on the outside by a wire gauze flap which opened upwards. This allowed the milkman to deliver the milk 'into' the house and for the housewife to take the bottles from the larder part of the cupboard without having to go outside. It was usually fitted to the coldest side of the house so that it could function as a rudimentary fridge. I also saw round the garden. Grandpa's green hut had been replaced by another one of a different colour but the same style. At the bottom of the garden, Arthur's Seat was in the same position as were the blackcurrant bushes although I rather doubt if they were the same plants.

Mr Jones remembered well the day his family decided to look at buying No. 57. His mother and sister and he were living at No. 28 Buccleuch Place and decided to walk down to see the house in Priestfield Road. He remembered that it was mainly Mrs Wilson who showed them round and on the second visit the price was agreed at £2,300. I asked Mr Jones particularly if he remembered my grandfather. He described him as a gentle, kindly man who had come from farming stock. When I asked how he was able to tell that my grandfather had spent his early years in the country, Mr Jones said 'because of the horseshoe'. Apparently when it came to the time to finalise the sale, Grandpa indicated that he was leaving the horseshoe behind as it had come from Galloway and belonged with the house called Cairnholy in Priestfield Road. Mr Jones allowed me to take a photograph of the horseshoe which looked to me as if it was intended for a fairly strong working horse. It had been nicely burnished and had the nail heads fused into the holes in the shoe. I have no idea when it first came into Grandpa's possession but he obviously treasured it, and it is just possible that it was handed to him by his mother and father as he was leaving Cairnholy to come to Edinburgh in 1900. Mementoes have a habit of turning up at the most unexpected times. Unfortunately, the name of the house, Cairnholy, had been lost some years ago when the glass fanlight above the door was accidentally broken by the heat of a blow-lamp being used to burn off paint. Any slight disappointment that there might have been at the loss of the name paled into insignificance when Mrs Jones contacted me a few days after my initial visit to say that her husband, Ted, had given the matter of the horseshoe a lot of thought and had come to the conclusion that the time was right for it to come back to the descendants of Joseph William Wilson. On 3 May 2004 I visited my grandfather's house for the second time in nearly 50 years and was presented with the horseshoe. Of all the situations which I have experienced during many months of researching the life of Joseph William Wilson, only the finding of the Creewood lintel stone has equalled the poignancy of those few moments with Elizabeth and Ted Jones.

Thoughts of Home

During the time that my grandparents were at Priestfield Road there was frequent contact with my grandfather's brothers and sisters who, by this time, had moved from Cairnholy to Kirkmabreck Farm and Blackmyre, a few miles into the hills. Indeed this family contact had gone on ever since Grandpa had left New Luce in 1900. The habit of visiting Cairnholy and Kirkmabreck had been passed down the generations so that members of the Cant family were also well aware of our roots on the Wilson side of the family. By contrast, there was no contact with, nor even any knowledge of, my grandmother's relatives, the Kains, at Dumfries, Hawick or Selkirk.

The Cant family and the Johnstone family visited Kirkmabreck for a short while in 1939 at the outbreak of the Second World War. This was in the nature of a voluntary evacuation in case of enemy action but as none materialised in Edinburgh at the start of the war, both the Cants and the

Granny Wilson with her first grandchild, Mary Johnstone, at Kirkmabreck farm house, 1933. *Courtesy of Mrs Mary Thomson, née Johnstone.*

At the back door of Kirkmabreck farm house in the mid-1920s, from left to right: William Wilson, Mrs Hamilton (a cousin of William Wilson), Annie Wilson, Agnes Wilson, John (Jeck) Wilson, Margaret (Peggie) Wilson. *Courtesy of Mrs Jean Stewart, née Wilson.*

Happy and relaxed 'amang my ain folk', at the front door of Kirkmabreck farm house, *c.* 1930. From left to right: George McIntosh Johnstone, Jean Johnstone, Grandpa Wilson, and his sister Annie Wilson. *Courtesy of Mrs Jean Stewart, née Wilson.*

Johnstones quickly returned home. At the time, the contingent consisted of Jean Johnstone and her daughters Mary and Sheila, and Annie Cant (my mother) and my sisters Mary and Grace. My introduction to the land of my maternal forebears was not until 1950 when I was a few weeks short of my 10th birthday. In those days, the Cant family (mother, father, four children and one to come) lived in a top flat tenement house at No. 39 Marchmont Crescent. From my perspective it was a sad house enlivened with occasional moments of joy. Outside the house, away from 'Unjust William', it was another world, never more exciting than in 1950 when my mother took us to Kirkmabreck Farm near Creetown. My father accompanied us to and from the holiday but for much of the intervening time he returned to Edinburgh to pursue his extra-curricular activities. In 1950 Kirkmabreck farm house was occupied by my great-uncle Willie (one of my grandfather's brothers), his wife Jean, and four of their six children: Tam; Annie; Minnie; and John. Two other daughters, Jean and Nancy, had already married and were living with their own families in Creetown and Pinmore, respectively. Another of my grandfather's brothers, John, or Jeck as he was usually called, lived with his wife, Jenny, in the dairy cottage beside the steadings. We lived in a small cottage without electricity or running water, which meant, of course, that we had to get used to the challenge of a dry toilet out in the garden.

The countryside and its people were so open and welcoming after the strictures of living in a tenement. I remember having an immediate affinity with the place, which has remained with me. That affinity might even have developed more quickly if I had been able to understand what my relatives were saying to me. The accent and the use of words that we had not even heard of made communication a major problem – at times anyway. Perhaps the easiest way to illustrate the problem is to narrate the circumstances leading up to my great-uncle Willie referring to me as a 'lying louse'. Up until then my veracity had never been impugned. Uncle Willie was driving the tractor and I was sitting on the trailer behind. We were coming from Blackmyre (where the sheep were being dipped) to Kirkmabreck, a distance of about two miles. The track was fairly rough and wet and before the days of cattle grids there were numerous gates on the route, especially near to the old Covenanters' kirkyard. I had learned that whoever was 'riding shotgun' needed to jump off the trailer when the tractor came to a gate, open it,

Outside the door of Kirkmabreck shepherd's cottage in the summer of 1950 where the Cant family lived for the entire school holidays. Back left to right: Grace Cant, Mary Cant, Malcolm Cant, and Anne Cant at the front. *Courtesy of Mrs Mary Sneddon, née Cant.*

allow the tractor through, close the gate again to keep the animals in, and jump back onto the trailer. The procedure had worked well until we got to the last gate where the track branched off to the quarry. Uncle Willie shouted that he wanted this gate kept open after we went through, but I found that the bottom rail of the gate was not catching on the rough grass verge and I could not get the gate to stay in the open position. Over the noise of the tractor I was being instructed to get 'a stane' and use it to hold the gate back. I became a bit flustered and went to move a stone which was far too big and looked as though it had been in the same position since the last Ice Age. I shouted back that I couldn't move it. By this time Willie was becoming less placid and shouted back over the noise of the engine '... lying louse'. Never in my life had I been referred to as a lying louse but fortunately the hurt and embarrassment lasted only a few moments when I heard a further instruction: 'that yin there, lying lowse'. I picked up the loose stone and pushed it under the gate. When I was older I wanted to tell Willie about the misunderstanding but I never quite summoned up the courage to do so.

During our stay at Kirkmabreck there was plenty of opportunity for my sisters and me to help in the fields either at hay-making or tattie-howking time. In those days, hay-making was a very labour-intensive job. Uncle Willie cut the grass with a long-bladed reaper pulled by the tractor.

LEFT. At Kirkmabreck farm house, in the early 1950s, left to right: William Wilson (brother of Joseph William Wilson), Georgina Wilson, Andrew Wilson, Annie Wilson, Kathleen Wilson, Ian Wilson and John Wilson. *Courtesy of William Taylor and Mrs Jean Watson.*

RIGHT. At Kirkmabreck farm house, *c.* 1955, standing left to right: Tam Wilson, John Wilson, Minnie Wilson, Annie Wilson, with their father and mother, Jean and William, seated. *Courtesy of Andrew Wilson.*

He started in one corner and went round and round the field finishing in the centre. After the cut grass had been turned a few times to dry it, the hay sweep, or 'tumblin-tam' as it was called, was used to draw all the hay into huge bundles ready to be built into rucks or miniature haystacks. As the rucks would have to stand in the field during wet weather they had to be skilfully built so that rain water ran off quickly and did not cause mould to start at the base. I remember my great-uncle Jeck's instructions: 'Pu' the butt, Malcolm, pu' the butt.' That entailed getting down on your hands and knees and removing the hay nearest to the ground to create a sort of drip bead for the rain to run off.

It was not, however, all work and no play. At the start of the holiday, my mother took us all to visit her cousins and also various aunts who had retired from farm life and were settled in Creetown. On each occasion, we were invited to tea which usually consisted of a meat salad followed by an assortment of home-baking. One of the longer journeys was to visit the Kennedy sisters, Agnes and Maggie, who ran the Post Office at Palnure

Palnure Post Office, Palnure, near Newton Stewart, with the name J. McGowan above the front door. Maggie Kennedy is on the left, and Agnes Kennedy is on the right. Seated is their aunt Jessie McGowan who handed over the running of the Post Office to her nieces shown in the picture. *Courtesy of Mrs Grace Thom, née Cant.*

near Newton Stewart. After we had had our tea and were looking round the house, we were suddenly aware of the presence of a fairly tall, serious-looking man, Tam Kennedy, who we all, rather unkindly, thought had just stepped down from a penny-farthing bicycle. Tam was the brother of Agnes and Maggie and was the village blacksmith. I remember in the hallway of the house he looked my father straight in the eye and said by way of introduction: 'And ur you a polis tae?' Some of us started to snigger at the thought of our father pounding the beat but were soon brought to heel by one of his disapproving looks. My father's reply: 'No, I am a schoolmaster', did nothing to encourage further small talk from the man who obviously thought that conversation should be limited to essential use only. We were later led to believe that the enquiry about my father's occupation had been a significant departure from normal practice. We had been greatly honoured – and amused.

The holiday ended all too soon and was marked on the final night by a family get-together in the parlour of the farm house. All the aunts and uncles and cousins and friends were there and huge quantities of sandwiches, scones, pancakes, biscuits and shortbread were brought in by my great aunt Jean, helped by her daughters Annie and Minnie. As the evening wore on and darkness fell, the paraffin lamps were brought through from the outer kitchen and a sing-song began. After a few solo items from Uncle Willie and others, the children were invited to do their turn but we were all too shy. Apparently such gatherings had happened for years. Jean Stewart (née Wilson) remembers that when she and her siblings and mother and father lived at Blackmyre there was always a family get-together at Kirkmabreck on New Year's Day. At the end of the evening, the family walked back to Blackmyre, a distance of about two miles with only a hurricane lamp to light their way. As they passed the Covenanters' moonlit graveyard no doubt their pace and heartbeat quickened.

At the end of the holiday we travelled back to Edinburgh by Western Omnibuses as far as Dumfries and then SMT to Edinburgh. Strangely, although we had enjoyed the holiday a great deal, I have no recollection of talking about it to my grandfather on our return.

THE CLOSING YEARS

For reasons which are still not at all clear, it was decided that my grandfather and grandmother, after selling their bungalow in Priestfield Road in 1956, would come and live with us at No. 31 Redford Loan. One of the theories in the family is that the pressure to move there came from my grandmother who was keen to be seen living in a nice new bungalow in Colinton. It was certainly an attractive house but it had only four principal rooms and was already full to overflowing with seven members of the Cant family. Even allowing for my grandmother being the prime mover, the arrangement could never have been implemented without the agreement of my father who was not in a position, financially, to be so accommodating. In assessing his generosity or otherwise I am reminded of the story told to me many years ago by one of his comrades who served with him in the Royal Scots during the Second World War. Apparently my father was the self-appointed 'manager' of the canteen where he dispensed, for a small consideration, cigarettes and soft drinks to the men. His tight grip on the financial side of the business earned him the sobriquet, 'Private Nowt for Nowt'.

Whatever the financial arrangements were, Granny and Grandpa Wilson arrived at Redford Loan and there was a major readjustment of the available space. For several months the arrangement seemed to work and I was never aware of a lot of open hostility, but in retrospect it is obvious that tensions were mounting and not being released. I remember the last night well. Low-level bickering quickly escalated when my grandmother suddenly launched into one of her frequent vicious tirades, making abusive

Granny and Grandpa Wilson at
No. 55 Priestfield Road (the
home of Jean and George
Johnstone) in October 1957.
Courtesy of Andrew Wilson.

comments about my mother, which were accompanied by physical assault.
Such behaviour, in the presence of the whole family, could result in only
one action – and that was immediate eviction. Within an hour or two, my
grandparents had come to the end of their short stay at Redford Loan.
Granny left in anger, Grandpa left in tears, and we were left in peace, or
perhaps pieces – for a while at least.

Although I was 17 years of age when my grandparents left our house
in 1957, I have no clear recollection of what happened thereafter. My
understanding is that they lived with the Johnstone family for a while at
No. 55 Priestfield Road, and then with John and Marion Wilson at West
Savile Terrace from about August 1957. What I do recall, however, is
learning in late 1957 that my grandfather had been admitted to the
Longmore Hospital with a serious heart attack. I remember a lot of coming
and going between the adults and hearing snippets of conversation about
my grandfather's deteriorating condition. His hospitalisation at the
Longmore could not have been more ironic. From his hospital bed he
could see the tenement building, and probably the windows, of No. 105
Causewayside where he was in digs with Mrs Fyfe's family in 1900 when he

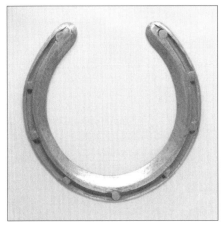

The Wilson horseshoe probably originated in Balmurrie or Cairnholy and was brought to Edinburgh by Joseph William Wilson. When Joseph sold No. 57 Priestfield Road in 1956, he gifted the horseshoe to the new owners, the Jones family, who kept it in the house for almost 50 years. Elizabeth and Ted Jones then kindly returned it to the descendants of Joseph William Wilson when they sold No. 57 in 2004. *Photograph by Douglas Hunter.*

first came to Edinburgh. I did not have a final conversation with my grandfather but I know that my sister Mary, who was carrying her first child at the time, promised her grandfather that if she gave birth to a boy, he would be called Joseph and if she gave birth to a girl, she would be called Josephine. Grandpa died at 1.40 pm on Thursday, 16 January 1958, and Mary and Danny Sneddon's first child, Josephine, was born on 17 August that year.

The funeral service for Joseph William Wilson was taken by the Rev. John Macintyre, the minister of Rosehall Church where Grandpa had been a member. The cortege left West Savile Terrace to drive the short distance to Newington Cemetery and turned in at the main gate from Dalkeith Road. The lair was at the south end of the driveway which runs parallel to Dalkeith Road. In those days only male members of a family went to the graveside which I think was a great injustice. Two of Grandpa Wilson's brothers, William and Jeck, of Kirkmabreck Farm, were to be cord-bearers. The brothers had made arrangements for William's son, John, to drive them to the funeral. The three men set off in good time but not far into the journey the weather worsened to the point where the road was completely blocked by snow. They phoned Edinburgh to say that, regrettably, they would not be able to attend the funeral which meant that the family had to re-arrange the allocation of cords. The absence of my grandfather's brothers at the funeral meant that my cousins, George Johnstone and Andrew Wilson and I had the honour of being cord-bearers at our grandfather's funeral.

EPILOGUE

Such then is the story of my grandfather, Joseph William Wilson, or, at any rate, all that I have been able to find out about him. When I compare the information gathered with my knowledge of Joseph before I started, it is tempting to think that the job is complete. But official forms only give us official information and do not go to the root of a person's character, aspirations or disappointments. On those topics, and many more, I think my research is incomplete as I simply did not find out how my grandfather thought about life or whether he was satisfied with what he had attained. Members of the present family will all have their private thoughts which cannot be adequately expressed in a small publication of this nature, but my overwhelming feeling is that he never lost his affinity with the land of his birth, and in coming to Edinburgh all those years ago, he probably felt quite isolated from his brothers and sisters.

During my research there were many moments of absolute boredom. Thumbing through volume after volume of Valuation Rolls, not knowing whether they were going to reveal even a modicum of relevant information, can only be described as character building. On the other hand I had remarkable runs of luck in the early stages of my research and even moments of joy and elation. I shall remember all my life the day Robert Horne of Drannandow phoned me to say that the Creewood lintel stone had been found and that I could come and collect it, and, later in the story, when Ted and Elizabeth Jones presented me with Joseph's horseshoe which had lain at No. 57 Priestfield Road for nearly half a century.

Joseph William Wilson was survived by his wife, Mary Jane Mathieson

Newington Necropolis was designed by David Cousin, the architect, and opened in 1844 by the Metropolitan Cemetery Association. The advertisements of the day carried the message 'Every information as to prices of Ground may be had on application to the Revd. David Crawford, the Secretary, at 3 Francis [Place] now Summer Hall Place'. The etching shows the vaults in the centre, behind which is the lodge house on Dalkeith Road. The background is Salisbury Crags and Arthur's Seat. From *The Post Office Edinburgh Directory 1846-47*.

Kain or Wilson by four years. The information unearthed on the Kain family was much more unexpected than that on the Wilsons. My grandmother did not give any indication to the present family of her upbringing in Dumfries, Hawick and Selkirk, even although we now know that there were many occasions when she had the opportunity to do so, especially in relation to Dumfries. None of us was aware, even, that she had come from a family of five. When she died at the Eastern General Hospital on 10 February 1962 the details of her early life, perhaps containing the reasons for her difficult character, died with her. I remember the day my grandmother was laid to rest beside my grandfather in Newington Cemetery. The family mourners stood in a semi-circle further from the grave than is customary. The cemetery staff had laid the coffin onto the battens above the open grave and the minister beckoned to the family to take up their positions beside the cords. No one moved. The minister again beckoned, but no one moved. He then signalled to the cemetery staff who came forward, untied the cords, and lowered Mary Jane to her final resting place: a sad end to a life which could, and should, have been much more enjoyable for herself and those around her, especially in her latter years.

During my attempt to reconstruct my grandfather's life I purposely delayed revisiting Newington Cemetery until most of my research was completed. I thought it would be the last simple act to find the grave and read again the family inscription. In fact it was very difficult to locate the grave as so many stones had been damaged or toppled. However, with the assistance of the cemetery staff I located lair 441 in Section I. The tombstone was lying on the ground, detached from the plinth, but not otherwise damaged. The inscription reads:

IN LOVING MEMORY OF
JOSEPH W. WILSON
DIED 16TH JANUARY 1958
AGED 78 YEARS
ALSO HIS WIFE
MARY KAIN
DIED 10TH FEBRUARY 1962
AGED 78 YEARS
ALSO THEIR CHILDREN
TOMMY AND MARY
WHO DIED IN INFANCY

In Newington Cemetery there are hundreds of similar tombstones in various states of repair. Some are more modest and some are much grander; but for sure they all have a story to tell.

The tombstone in Newington Cemetery marking the burial place of Joseph William Wilson and his wife Mary Kain, and their two children, Tommy and Mary, who died in infancy. *Photograph by Phyllis M. Cant.*

INDEX